monsoonbooks

JASMINE FEVER

New York chef Frank Visakay traveled around the world twice before settling in Thailand, where he now lives with his constant companion Louke Chai, a handsome German Shepherd, and his faithful Harley-Davidson—more a work of art than a form of transport—which he keeps in his living room.

Visakay is the author of *Everything But Die*, and co-author of *Adventure Cambodia*. He is currently writing his third novel.

T0159435

JASMINE FEVER

FRANK VISAKAY

monsoon

monsoonbooks

Published in 2007
by Monsoon Books Pte Ltd
52 Telok Blangah Road
#03-05 Telok Blangah House
Singapore 098829
www.monsoonbooks.com.sg

ISBN-13: 978-981-05-8973-8
ISBN-10: 981-05-8973-5

Cover illustration copyright © Tan Hong Yew

Printed in Singapore

12 11 10 09 08 07   1 2 3 4 5 6 7 8 9

Contents

Jasmine Fever

On his way home on night, my friend Danny stopped at the Happy Bar in Karon for a drink. It was a quiet night for a change and he ordered his usual Sang Som and soda. There was a figure slumped over the far end of the bar. His head was down and one arm stretched out lifelessly. Even from this distance the man looked entirely disheveled. It was hard to tell but he looked strangely familiar. Danny picked up his drink and slowly approached the slovenly figure.

My God, it was his friend Mac. Danny sat down next to him, wondering how he was going to get the guy home. Just pick him up and take him, he supposed. God, he looks like hell. He's been here three days, I bet, just laying on the bar like that.

Danny pushed away the empty bottle of Mekong and wiped away the cigarette butts and ashtray. He put his arm around his friend and lifted him to his feet. 'Mac, wake up. Time to go home.'

Mac lifted up his head. His face was covered in stubble and his breath stank of booze and stale cigarettes. He stared at Danny through unfocused eyes. 'What happened? I know she loved me. I just don't know what happened,' he mumbled.

'Looks like Jasmine Fever is what happened, pal. Time to go home now.' Danny hoisted Mac up and headed towards the silver Toyota with his friend muttering every step of the way. He eased Mac into the passenger's seat and walked around to the driver's side of the car in time to see his friend Peter heading towards him.

'Holy smokes, what happened to Mac?'

'A bad case of Jasmine Fever.'

'What's that?'

'It's like getting malaria and dengue at the same time. Comes on all at once and there's not much you can do about it. First it affects your heart then goes into your brain. You start having wild delusions, imagining all kinds of things. You lose all sense of reason, start acting irresponsibly and behaving strangely. Usually newcomers to the Kingdom are the most susceptible but I've seen guys here eight or ten years come down with it.'

'Wow, sounds bad. Is there a cure?'

'No, there's no cure. It just has to run its course. It can leave you a battered and broken man. Just look at old Mac here. Well, if you catch it early, there's a slight chance. What you have to do is stick your head in a bucket of cold water every morning, drink a cup of strong black coffee and smack yourself in the face a few times.'

'How did Mac get it?'

'It shouldn't have happened to him. He's been coming to Phuket on vacation every year for the past six years. He should have known better. What he told me was the last thing he remembers is strolling down the beach in the moonlight holding hands with his Thai girlfriend. She reached up and put both arms around his neck and told him that she loved him more than anything in the world. He remembers the sound of the waves and the smell of jasmine in the air. That night, after a round of great sex, she wrapped her hard, twenty-three-year-old body around him and said that she wanted to take care of him and stay with him for the rest of her life, if only she could find a way to support her mother after she quit working in the bars.

'It was the anaesthesia that did it,' continued Danny. 'The insensitivity to pain or anything else, like common sense for instance, artificially induced by the nearness of her intentions. That's it, of course, your brain goes numb. They stand so close that they breathe in all the oxygen and exhale nitrous oxide right into your lungs. The kind of gas the dentists use. I used to love that stuff, just float along as happy as can be. When that Thai girl stands close and touches you and whispers into your ear, that's it, you're finished. It's Jasmine Fever time.

'The next day he woke up and had full on Jasmine Fever. He thought that he could live happily ever after with a Thai bargirl. He went out and bought a restaurant for half a million baht, put it in her name, the poor guy. Two weeks before the grand opening she went out and bought a big stereo system and a television too. Spent a fortune—his money, of course. He hit the roof, started to argue with her that it was too much money to spend. She picked up the phone and called the police. She had him thrown out of the place. He couldn't believe it. You know how big Mac is, don't you? Well a little Thai cop, must have weighed 100 pounds soaking wet, came and shoved handcuffs into Mac's face. Said if he ever saw him on the streets again, or if he ever set foot on the property, he would take him to the airport and put him on the first plane out of there. He's been at the bar ever since. Can't figure out what happened. But enough of this, it's too depressing. What about you? What have you been up to?'

Peter hesitated a bit. 'Funny that you ask. I've decided to move my girlfriend in with me. She's going to quit her job on Soi Sea Dragon and live with me. She's really a very sweet girl and wants to stop working in the bars. She's a good girl, not like the rest of them.'

'Hey, Peter. You know that I'm your friend, don't you? And that I love you like a brother,' said Danny, taking a step closer.

'Yeah?'

Danny grabbed Peter by the shirt and slapped him hard in the face, twice, with his open hand. Smack! Smack!

'Well then, wake up, for God's sake.'

Can Leopards
Change their Spots?

I met Jay while I was having lunch in Don's Restaurant. He was American, about fifty years old and seemed to be a number one nice guy. He introduced me to his 'wife' and two children, a Thai boy and girl about eight and nine years old. He told me he was having a house built down the street. He was a happy camper.

His lady friend looked like she had just stepped off a stage in Patpong. She was covered in gold, had long red nails and lots of make-up. She spoke good English and seemed to be a sharp cookie. You could tell. Some Thai girls were just not interested in what was going on or couldn't care less, just sitting there passing the time of day, kind of sleepy-looking—but not this one. She was alert and you could tell.

I ran into Jay a few times at Don's after that and we became friends. He confided that he had not been in Thailand very long and had just met his lady friend in Bangkok but considered her his wife and he felt like a father to her two children. He had enrolled her two kids in Dulwich School. This is serious money we're talking here. His house was costing eight million baht and, of course, it would be in her name. If anything happened to him, he wanted her to be provided for. I figured he had some good money stashed away. He had run his own accounting business and had sold it with an agreement that he would not take his clients with him. I wasn't worried about Jay. He seemed to have it all together. The house was built and they moved in.

I ran into Jay a few months later at Don's. He was slumped

in his seat, his head in his hands. I sat down across from him. We often ate together. He stared at me—or rather, through me. He looked as if he hadn't slept in days.

'Jay, what is it?' I touched his arm.

'My wife wants to leave me. She's bored. She wants to back to Bangkok. I don't know what to do.' I knew better than to ask what she was going to do in Bangkok.

'Christ, is that all? I was afraid someone had died or something. Consider yourself lucky. Help her pack and count your blessings.'

Hey, I can give advice to my friends at the drop of a hat. However, not all of it is appreciated or even noticed. Jay agreed to meet me the next day. I wanted to help him through this transition. And indeed, the next day he looked great.

'Hi, Jay. What's up?' I was happy to see him looking so well.

'Nothing to worry about. I've got everything straightened out. I'm going back to work in America and I will leave the house to my wife and she's going to rent it out for 35,000 a month. That will take care of everything. When I get some money saved, I'll come back and she's going to wait for me.'

'Christ, Jay. I thought you were solvent.' (This guy's an accountant? I thought)

'I spent more than I intended to. I need to build up some cash.' I shook his hand and wished him the all the best.

A few weeks later I was in the queue at Siam Commercial Bank and who was right in front of me but Jay's 'wife'. She didn't look anxious to talk to me. Okay, no matter. I noticed she was holding a fat stack of silver notes in her hand. She passed them and a bank book over to the teller. I just couldn't help myself. I had to kind of stand on my toes when the teller placed all those thousand-baht bills in a counting machine. The green light lit up: seventy. That was 70,000 baht.

I pondered this for a day or two until I ran into a mutual

friend.

'Hey, Jay's wife struck it rich. She moved in with some German. He bought her a brand new pick-up truck and he's giving her 70,000 a month. Can you believe it?'

I could believe it as I'd seen her a few day's before making a deposit. That and the house rental money would be a nice income for her.

Jay came back a year later and she contrived to move into a little dumpy shack with her sister. I ran into them, and Jay was happy and still in love. The girl gave me a look—like 'go ahead, I dare you to say something'. She didn't have to worry about me. I have to live here and live is the operative word. She convinced Jay to take her to Bangkok for the month that he was there so as not to run into her new 'husband'.

My question is: how good do you have to treat these girls to make them happy? Is it even possible?

A few years ago a Frenchman bought two *rai* of land down the street from me and built a small house and an outdoor bar. It was large, round and had a thatched roof. He planned to have a kitchen and serve food. He had a row of rooms constructed along one side of the property—about ten of them so he could have girls do massages.

Why? Because he had a bargirl in Patong that had just had his baby and he was going to start a new life for them. We stopped in for drinks a few times and it was a pleasant place, away from the traffic and noise and no thump-thump music. Very nice.

We never did get to eat there though. His girlfriend got bored out of her mind and left him and the baby. Just disappeared into the night, or should I say nightlife. The Frenchman sold the place and moved back to France with his new baby.

About four years back there was a nice-looking man, about thirty-five years old. He bought a beautiful outdoor restaurant on Wiset Road in Rawai for his girlfriend. The restaurant claimed to serve French food. It had loungers and plush, brightly colored sofas. Very pretty and would not have looked out of place in the middle of Bangkok.

The most breathtaking sight in the entire place was his girlfriend. She was a knockout. She was sophisticated and smart. I mean smart in a fashion sense. I used to have a drink there just to see the girl—not that she was bothered with me. She was drop-dead gorgeous. She also looked like she would be more comfortable with a chrome pole to hold onto but heck, if she'd asked me I would have bought her a bar, a house, and a car, anything that she wanted. But she had the look of a traveler and a traveler she was.

The problem is that Rawai is a sleepy little town. Not much going on here. The action starts in Patong and runs down the hill to Karon then Kata. By the time it gets to Chalong and Rawai, there's nothing happening. You can shoot off a cannon in the streets at night and not hit anything. After being a hostess in a restaurant with no business for two or three months, the girl became bored silly and one day she did a runner.

Now her boyfriend, as I said, was a very nice-looking guy. He could have recovered nicely. I doubt very much if he ever had trouble getting girls. What did he do? He hung himself from a large tree in front of his house.

But enough of this. It's too depressing.

What does one have to do here to feel secure, to make your girlfriend stay, to make her happy? You give her everything you possibly can—your love, your heart, your time, your money—and it still doesn't work.

The moral of these stories?

Leopards do not change their spots. They eat you alive.

More Wild
Animal Stories

Lately I have been daydreaming of having a girl give me a shower in the morning, washing me down, sleeping with me naked at night. I have been thinking of having a Thai girl move in with me. Possibly she could just walk around my house in skimpy clothes and I could look at her. Reach out and touch her. I'm a lover of beauty. There's nothing wrong with that or in wanting a bit of companionship.

However, one should know exactly what one is getting into and have no illusions when a Thai girl moves in. Physical stuff: nice body, cleanliness, sweet-smelling, terrific-looking, smiley, cooking and cleaning. They're good at that.

Brain power? Don't count on it. Could I have someone to talk to and keep me company? Don't be silly. This is an unreasonable expectation, I told myself. One soon tires of mono-syllabic conversations. Ask any Thai bargirl where a street is or a business or a building, even if it's only a few blocks away, how to get somewhere, what they think about what's happening in the government or any kind of question that requires just a little thought. They have no idea whatsoever. What can you expect of someone who passes the time by lounging around all day, zoning out and staring into space? If they really get ambitious, they read a comic book.

Talk about the future—it's not here yet and the past has gone, hasn't it? There is only today and not much doing at that—nothing stirring in their simple minds except how to transfer cash from your ATM to theirs.

Then I think back to the few times that I did have a Thai girl living with me. One quit the bar that she was working at and gave me a few free days. I moved her in with a monthly salary. Every time we went shopping, she had to have something, anything, no matter what it was, and I bought it for her.

She said she could only stay for three months and when high season came she had to go back to work and make some real money. The three months passed and I was wondering when she was going to leave. One night I got drunk and told her that I loved her and did not want her to go back to the bar.

The next morning I woke up and had completely forgotten what I'd said. Obviously she hadn't as she asked me for 20,000 baht. She wanted to get her eyes made rounder or something. I refused. Christ, she was costing me enough as it was.

'Okay, you no give me money I go back to bar.'

What the hell was this? I thought. I was angry as I had been giving her anything she wanted. It was not until later in the afternoon that I remembered what I had said the night before and how it must have seeped into her feeble little brain and stayed there. It was partly my fault.

'Are you sure?' I said.

'Yes. I go bar.'

'Are you sure?'

'Yes. You no give money—I go bar.'

I got up from my computer, grabbed her small suitcase and a few large black plastic garbage bags and started dumping her crap in them, including the new tennis racquet that she had wanted.

I put her and her stuff in the car and drove to Kata. It wasn't far. Halfway there she started crying and saying she did not want to go back, that she was only joking, sobbing her eyes out. I almost felt like turning the car around, but the decision was made. I pulled up to the bar, threw the bags out on the street and sailed her tennis racquet as far away as I could.

A few years later, not having learned my lesson, I moved another cute little thing in. After three months I was going crazy. She would not let me out of her sight. If I took the dogs for a walk on the beach she had to go. I could take a ride on my Harley at any time, even visit a girly bar, but she had to be right there. After a few more months I told her I couldn't stand it. She had to leave.

'Christ, I can't even go to the bathroom alone,' I shouted at her.

'Okay you can, no problem.' I shook my head. I would have to be more specific.

'Get out! Pack up and leave.'

'I have nowhere to go. I love you. I want stay here.'

'I am going to pick up your stuff and throw it and you over the fence.'

'Go ahead. I call police. Tell them you rape me.'

'That's ridiculous. You're a bargirl and have been living here for months.'

'I'm a Thai girl. Police also Thai. Who they believe? Tonight you sleep in jail.'

Jesus Christ, she had a point. A Mexican stand-off.

After a week of hard negotiations we settled on me giving her 18,000 baht to help her 'find a new life': meaning a new man and the money would tide her over. Okay, I could have paid more or paid less but at the time it looked like the only way I would get rid of her.

As one friend said (and I wish I could remember who it was), 'You don't pay them 1,000 or 2,000 to come to your house. You are actually paying them to leave in the morning.'

Case closed.

I have my two beautiful dogs to keep me company and I talk to them all of the time. They really try to listen to me and hear what I am saying, I swear. They obey me without question. Wait home at the gate for me to return. I am absolutely sure of their love for me.

And these are the only two animals that I will have live with me.

Yes, you're right. I attribute it to the *Seven Year Itch* syndrome. You remember the movie with Tom Ewell and Marilyn Monroe? It is based on the premise that after seven years of marriage, the relationship is diminished.

Bangkok Love

'Take me to Patpong,' he told the cab driver.

'Patpong closed now. I take you to better place—private club, many nice girls there.'

'Cut the crap. I know it's open.'

'Okay, 500 baht.'

'No way, put on the meter.' The American had not been to Bangkok before, but he was smart. After all, he lived in New York City and cab drivers were the same all over the world. It wasn't as if he was from the middle of Iowa or someplace.

Patpong was a street crowded with souvenir stands, food vendors and bars. No one could actually drive down the street as the real estate was so expensive. Every square inch of space was used to sell one thing or another. Mostly there were bars. Bars with brightly colored neon signs one after the other: Girls a-Go-Go, Pretty Girl, Pink Palace. Names even more graphic, winking and glowing in different colors, calling out to you.

There were hawkers on the crowded street pushing their places, shouting, 'You want see show?' Shoving photos of nude women towards people passing by; all kinds of photos: girls putting in or taking out unimaginable things from their private parts or women embracing each other in the most suggestive poses. The American was experienced enough to know that these particular dives were rip-off joints and he kept walking.

There were so many bars that it was hard to know which one to go into, but he imagined that most of the go-go bars were pretty much the same. He walked into one of them. It was dark and the music was loud and pounding. The air conditioner was working great and it was nice and cool inside. There was a stage along one wall with about twenty girls dancing in place, swaying back and forth to the music. Some were moving slowly and some more quickly. Others were grinding and humping imaginary lovers on the stage, writhing like kite tails in a strong wind. There were dozens of booths and the American slipped into an empty seat and looked around. The place was mostly full of single white males intently watching the dancers. Many of them had their hands on the legs of go-go girls sitting next to them. Most of the men drank beer and all of the girls were drinking coke or orange juice. The American knew that these were called 'girly drinks' and you were expected to purchase one if you wanted company at your table. A waitress came over and he ordered a drink.

He sipped his drink and scanned the stage. There was a stunning girl at the far end, towards the back. She looked as if she was lost and had wandered onto the stage by some strange accident. She was certainly embarrassed to be there. She was the most beautiful girl that he had ever seen. You would think that the management would put a girl like that right out at the front. He couldn't stop staring at her. Mostly she kept her head down and diverted her eyes from the staring crowd, but she did notice him and smiled a small shy smile.

When the music stopped, some of the girls came down from the stage and others excused themselves from their customers and went up to dance. The girl walked tentatively in his direction. He waved her over, palm down as he had read in the guidebook.

'My name Sai. What name you?'

The American told her. She slipped into the booth and sat close. Her long dark hair fell over her bare shoulders and down past her large breasts which were scarcely contained by a bikini top. He thought that she had the quality of a ripe peach, bursting with fresh sweetness.

'Would you like a drink?' the American asked.

'Oh, thank you.' She threw her arms around his neck. Her skin was firm and warm and she smelled of lavender. He felt her tremble. She started to cry softly, her tears spilling down her face and touching his cheek.

'I'm forced to work here. My father borrow much money from owner to pay gambling debts. Now I must have sex with many customers to pay my father's loan. I never go with man before.'

'Why don't you just quit?'

'I have no one to stay with, have no money. You are so handsome man. I wish I could stay with you.'

'I have to go back home to New York City at the end of the week.'

'I can go with you.'

'What would I have to do?' As he spoke, his voice caught in his throat and his heart raced with the thought of it.

'I must repay my father's loan. Then I'm free. I can stay with you long time. I would give anything go to America.' She put her head down and sighed, as if it were an impossible dream.

'How much do you owe?'

'One hundred thousand baht.'

He silently calculated the amount. It came to over US$2,000. He had brought just a little more than that. He had wanted to be sure that he had enough money with him when he traveled. This could work, he thought. It was good luck, a matter of being in the right place at the right time and having the brains to realize it. She was as sweet as apple pie and his friends back home would fall on the floor when they saw her.

He endorsed his travelers check and gave them to the bar owner. He insisted on and received a receipt. As a New Yorker, he knew the importance of doing business correctly.

He and Sai left the bar and flagged down a cab. She rested her head on his shoulder and hugged him all the way back to his hotel. He had a luxury suite at the Marriott on Soi Two, Sukhumvit. As they entered his room, she exclaimed, 'Oh my darling, I was so happy to be going with you, I wasn't thinking. I forgot my clothes and shoes at the bar. I must go back for them.'

'Not now, we'll go tomorrow. I want to keep you here with me.'

'No, I never want to see that place again. I want to be finished. Never think of it again. Please, you can give me only 300 baht for cab and I'll be able to get everything. I need my toothbrush and comb and things. I come right back to you. Run water in tub and put in lots of bubbles. I will be back in a flash.' She kissed him fully and lovingly on the mouth.

'It be okay, you have drinks sent up for us?' She asked in a soft, shy voice. The American turned on the water in the tub and called room service. He sat on the bed to wait, filled with happiness, dreaming of her return, thinking of that first naked glimpse of her. But Sai did not return.

After two hours, he grabbed a cab and went back to Patpong. He was worried about her. Maybe she'd had an argument with the owner or had been mugged. It was after two in the morning and the bar on Patpong was closed, along with the rest of the bars and stores. He could not sleep. The American pulled the phone book out from the desk near the bed and called the local police, then all of the nearby hospitals. No one had heard of a girl named Sai. The American opened his laptop, punched in Google and then Thailand. First he looked for agencies that might help. Then he read about Thailand in general. He read until the sun came through his window, then he read some more.

He went to the bar. It was the only way that he could think of to try and find her. The door was ajar and an old lady was sweeping the floor. 'Not open. You come back eight o'clock tonight.'

The American spent an anxious day walking the streets, stopping every now and then for a drink. He could only hope that Sai was all right. He arrived at the bar shortly after eight. The room was as dark as before and he saw her sitting at a table with a very fat white man. Sai was wearing the same skimpy outfit. The man had one huge flabby arm around her. He was wearing a sleeveless T-shirt and the fatness of his body seemed to pour out of the sides of his shirt. As the American walked towards the table, Sai reached over and hugged the man. The American heard her say, 'I'm forced to work here. You are so handsome man. I wish I could stay with you.'

The American ignored them and kept on walking. He found the owner. 'See that girl over there?' He nodded towards Sai. 'I gave you 100,000 baht last night. I want it back.'

The owner started speaking harshly in Thai, punching a thick finger into the American's chest. Two large Thais appeared on either side of the American, standing very close. The American reached into his pocket just as the Thais grabbed him roughly by the arms. He could just about grasp the 500-baht note. 'Let's all have a drink, talk things over.'

They sat down at a table. The American began quietly. 'You spoke English very well last night, so let's continue that way.' He idly put a cell phone on the table and spun it with one finger while he spoke. 'Do you know who I am or why I am in Bangkok? Just another stupid *farang* you can take advantage of?' The American smiled. The Thai didn't answer. He just shrugged his shoulders and stared at the American as if he was a bug he might squash with one fat fist. The American stopped his expensive cell phone from spinning, letting it come to rest so that the screen faced the bar owner. When the American punched a button, the words phone book appeared. He touched another button.

The name of a Member of Parliament appeared. He was one of the richest and most powerful men in Thailand. He was also in control of the entire Khlong Toey district, including Patpong. No merchandise entered or left the port without his permission, not a container ship or even a bag of rice. Every business had to pay tribute without exception. Dissident merchants were dealt with swiftly and harshly. Mothers told their children to behave or the General would come for them.

'If I touch that button again, it starts to ring. Or I can speak to my very close friend at our business meeting tomorrow. We're having lunch at The Oriental Hotel. They say that the atmosphere there is quite luxurious and serene. It would be a pity to ruin the mood by having to tell the General that I, his dear friend, was robbed on my very first night in his country. His loss of face would be great. Imagine his anger, his rage.' The American shuddered at a thought too horrible to contemplate.

He paused for what seemed like a very long time. 'Or we can just forget all about this misunderstanding. Up to you.' The American shrugged his shoulders. 'I took the liberty of dropping off a letter explaining everything at The Oriental. It's addressed to myself and the General. If I were you I would pray to God that nothing happens to me tonight and that I arrive early enough tomorrow to retrieve the letter before the General has a chance to open it.' He sipped his drink, still smiling.

The Thai bar owner pushed his chair back, its force almost knocking over the table. He came back a few minutes later and slammed a handful of money in front of the American who calmly counted it. It was 100,000 baht all right. The American looked up at the Thai. 'You're 50,000 short.'

The bar owner cried out in rage, pounded on the table, his face inches from the American's, and let out a string of curses in Thai.

The American turned his head to the side. 'Christ, your breath stinks. Look, this is Thailand and you know everything costs money. Do you want to get this over with or not?' As the owner headed behind the bar again, the American called out, 'Don't be flattered into thinking that your miserable life is worth 50,000 baht. No one would bet a single *satang* on your living another hour should my friend become aware of your misdeeds. You'll be feeding the fish and this dump will be bulldozed into rubble all in the same day. Do not throw the money down again like that. Don't you know the King's picture is on those bills? You disrespectful fat buffalo.'

The Thai came back with the 50,000 and placed it on the table. The American put it in his pocket without counting. He knew it would all be there. He walked towards the door, hardly glancing at Sai who, by now, had her roly-poly mark firmly under her spell.

'Throw out the fat *farang* and dump the girl. She's finished here,' the American called out as he left the bar and stepped onto the small *soi*.

It was a beautiful warm night and a slight breeze cooled the air. Maybe Bangkok wasn't so bad after all and heck, he might just go and have lunch one day at The Oriental after all. A table on the riverside terrace would be very pleasant.

The American tossed the cell phone into the first garbage receptacle that he found. After all, he was on vacation and there was no one in Thailand that he knew anyway. Amazing the information one could find on Google.

Journey of Love

Sumalin is the most beautiful girl in Phuket. She has the hard body of an athlete and the skin the color of crème caramel. She looks into your eyes when she speaks to you as if you are the most important person in the world. She has a sparkling smile and full sensuous lips that seem to be on the verge of telling you a secret that only the two of you can share.

I am madly in love with her and we have been close for the past year. There are only two things that we really disagree about.

Firstly, I want to marry her as soon as possible but she keeps saying that she is not ready. Secondly, she loves motorcycles while I dislike them immensely. I prefer my automobile and the safety of four wheels, but she drives all over on her 450cc Honda. There are over 10,000 reported road accidents a year in Phuket, an enormous amount, and most involve motorbikes. When I drive down the highway it reminds me of a video game, where moving objects come at you from all sides. Winning the game means avoiding being hit. I hate riding on two wheels and only drive my little Honda Dream when my car is in for repairs, having been run into three times by speeding kids on motorbikes: once when I was waiting at a light, another time when I was parked, and the last time when a kid raced past me and tore off my side-view mirror.

Sumalin and I were watching television one evening when a story came on about the annual car and motorcycle show in Bangkok. The highlight of the affair was the fastest production motorcycle in the world—a Suzuki Hayabusa with air-blown fuel injection. The engine was black steel instead of the usual chrome and aluminum. It generated 175 horsepower, more than three small Japanese cars combined. It had small handlebars, a short wheel base and clean lines with not one ounce of extra ornamentation. The term 'brute force' leapt to my mind as I looked at it. Even I could appreciate the potency of this extraordinary but dangerous-looking machine.

'Oh my God,' said Sumalin. 'I'd do anything to have that motorcycle.'

'Anything? If I bought it would you marry me?' I asked, only half in jest.

'No, I wouldn't. But the day you buy it and give it to me, we will drive to my mother's house to ask her permission and the next day we will go to the temple and be married.'

'Okay, but only if we go in my car.'

We both laughed and went back to watching the screen.

That night I couldn't sleep. I tossed and turned and woke up early. When the morning came I found myself on a plane to Bangkok. I was determined to buy the motorcycle, give it Sumalin and be married in a matter of days. I landed at Suvarnabhum Airport and took a cab directly to the Queen Sirikit Convention Center all the way on the other side of town. The show was still on and I could purchase the motorcycle on the spot as soon as the show was over at the end of the week. I had to raise over three million baht in a matter of days. It would be worth every penny to see the expression on Sumalin's face when I handed her the keys.

I called my attorney, sold all of my stocks and cashed in my retirement fund. The only bad news was that, after paying the customs duty and registration fees, I didn't have money left to have the machine shipped to Phuket. I would have to take the long drive myself and I wasn't looking forward to it.

I started early the next day, accompanied by visions of Sumalin in a Thai silk wedding dress. Halfway home I stopped at a traffic light on the highway. Three Harley Davidsons pulled up alongside me, all chrome and custom painted. Hot-shot oil riggers with money to burn on hopped-up cycles, gunning their engines and edging up as the light started to change.

What the heck, I'll just try it, I thought as I came up even with them. They glanced in my direction and smirked, revving their engines even more. The lights changed and we were off, our back wheels spinning and smoking in protest. I rocketed ahead, the front wheel leaving the ground as I shifted into second gear. I quickly sped past the fat hogs and kept on going.

I tailgated a Porsche Carrera and blew my horn for the passing lane. I could see the driver smile as he glanced in the rear-view mirror and stomped on the gas. I opened up and leaned forward over the tank as the awesome power between my legs surged through my entire body. The machine and I blended into one being as we shot past the car in a single swift and fluid motion.

By the time I reached Phuket it was too late to go to Sumalin's house. I would take her the bike first thing in the morning. She was really going to love it. I stopped at the Safari Club for a fast drink and when I came out, the Suzuki was surrounded by people. It wasn't a beautiful bike but you could sense its raw power. It was like a sleeping panther that could awake at any moment.

The girls begged me for rides and the guys asked me questions about the engine and bikes in general, as if I would naturally know the answers. The machine had a magic of its own.

I drove out towards the airport. There was a quarter-mile strip marked off on the highway by a motorcycle club and they raced late at night, for fun and for money. The bets were as high as 20,000 baht. I won every heat and left with a pocket full of cash.

I opened the throttle and turned the calm summer air into a gale-force wind that screamed siren songs through my helmet and forced me back, hard against the seat. The trees melted into a blur of Monet landscapes and the roar of my exhausts blotted out the entire world. Bright white stars grew larger in the sky as I flew into the night. I was the most powerful man on earth.

That was three weeks ago. I am going to give the Suzuki to

Sumalin any day now and we'll be married soon. But first I want to go to Ko Samui, take some cash from those bad-boy bikers over there, clean them out and leave them crying; and maybe the week after I'll check out the racers up in Bangkok. My Suzuki will chew them up and spit out crumpled chrome and rust. Then I'll park in front of the big nightclubs and watch people's reactions when they see my bike.

It's Okay to Play as Long as You Know the Rules

Is everyone else thinking what I'm thinking when they hear some of these bargirl stories?

The ones by the Desperate Dans and the stories where the guys say that they spent two and a half million baht on their Thai girlfriend and it still wasn't enough. And the story by the kid who loves this bargirl but knows their relationship is hopelessly in the toilet and now he wants to achieve the unachievable and turn her heart around. All the *farang*s that buy businesses for their girlfriends or purchase houses in their names and loose everything. The guy that comes here on vacation and then sends a monthly stipend to some girl he met in a bar so she can quit the business.

She's different, of course. Not like the other bargirls; she really wants to quit the life and go home to her mother, if only she had a monthly income. 'I'll stay home and wait for you. I promise.'

I feel so sorry for these men, don't you? You must do. What's going on? What's the matter with these guys? Where do they come from? Ohio? Have they been out of the house lately?

Well, yes, we do know. It's Jasmine Fever, of course. Anyone can catch it. You are cognizant of this if you have been in Thailand for a while. Older guys who haven't spoken to a female in years and young guys who don't know any better are all falling head over heels in love. I'm not blaming them or disparaging them. It's so very easy here to let your heart run away with your head.

Almost impossible not to, isn't it?

Personally, I'm all for it—falling in love with a bargirl,

spending your money on hookers, having as much fun as possible. Imagine a twenty-year-old beauty wrapped around you all night. Sounds wonderful to me, and it is. As my friend Dennis Pitman said when quoting Tom Clancy, 'I believe that sex is one of the most beautiful, natural, wholesome things that money can buy.'

Do you remember Heidi Fleiss? She was the Beverly Hills, California madam that got busted for sending prostitutes to rich guys and movie stars. After all the news stories, the trial and all of the publicity, what I remember most is Charlie Sheen. You know, the son of Martin Sheen. Charlie is a movie star and a very handsome man. I am sure that he has no trouble getting women. Well, according to news reports, he spent US$20,000 with Heidi's service. He would have girls dress up as cheerleaders and go over to his house. He didn't need to do this; he was just enjoying life. What I remember most is being impressed that he spent US$20,000. I stood up and shouted, 'Atta way to go, Charlie!'

The term 'sex tourist' is bandied about and used way too often. I'm tired of hearing this phrase from all sides. Most of the men coming here are not sex tourists. God, I hate that word and that's the last time that I'm going to use it. Men coming to Thailand are looking for a girlfriend experience. They are looking for love and acceptance; the warmth and nearness of a naked female body alongside them at night. This is the nicest escapade that one can have. What can be better than this? Watching soccer playoffs? Driving a Harley or a Ferrari? Eating Beluga caviar and drinking Krug champagne? Don't make me laugh. Nothing in life matches the experience and the closeness of love with a beautiful girl.

So what's the problem? Why am I writing all of this? Now, listen to me! Write this down and tape it onto your mirror. Better yet, cut and paste the title of this chapter. Print it out. It's already in capital letters as it should be. Read it every day that you are in Thailand.

No, no, I am not talking to you, you know who you are

and what you are doing. I want to tell the rest of you something brilliant that my dear friend Matt Jacobson told me.

Matt said, 'It's okay to play as long as you know the rules.'

Think about it. This one sentence gives you personal permission to do whatever you want, spend whatever you want and fall in love as many times as you want—with whoever you like—as long as you remember the rules!

The rules are that you are here to have as much fun as you can and the girls are here to take as much money from you as they can. It's that simple. The demimondaines (thanks Mr Trink) are just doing their job and they're pretty good at it, aren't they?

Do I think that those two lithe beauties I plucked off the stage at Pretty Lady, took back to my hotel then flew to Phuket—business class no less—with me for the weekend, loved me?

Of course not.
Did I love them?
Of course not.
Did I have a terrific time?
You bet I did.
Were they financially rewarded?
You bet they were.

Think of it like this. Imagine that you just stepped off the boat in a foreign country. As you walk down the pier you see four men playing cards. They wave you over and ask you to join them.

'What are you playing ?' you ask.

They mention a game that you have never heard of.

'What are the rules and how do you play?'

'Don't worry, you'll learn as you go along,' they say.

Now, do you take a seat and plunk down a stack of your hard-earned cash? No, you do not. And why is that? Because you don't know the rules and you are not stupid.

Now, you are smart enough not to put your money on the table and enter a game where you don't know the rules, so don't do it here either.

Gentlemen, come on, engage in all the revelry that you want in Thailand and have a tremendous amount of pleasure but remember this: it's okay to play as long as you know the rules.

When you play—and lose sight of the rules—you are one dead duck.

How Does it Happen?

Dan's eyes were open. He stared at the fluorescent light on the ceiling. When do they turn? he wondered. Does it happen all at once or are there signposts along the way? Suppose they are that way all along and you just don't know it? Is there a way to tell? There probably is: that first time they get a crazed look in their eyes after a few Sang Soms; or when they say, 'No, you can not go without me.'

He was fifty-five years old and this tiny Thai girl was telling him what he could and couldn't do. How strange, he thought. But he didn't pay much attention the first few times it happened. Maybe it was the night a few weeks after she'd moved in, when they ate at the little restaurant on Rawai Beach. It was a beautiful night, the sun had just set, and the sky was purple and orange. Dan was in love with his new girlfriend and was feeling that all was well with the world.

'I see you look girl,' Noi exclaimed.

'What girl?' Dan asked.

Enraged, Noi swept the plates from the table. Dan stared at his noodles flung across the bamboo carpet as she stomped out. He was puzzled, and later that evening asked Noi what had happened, why had she behaved like that. He knew that she loved him very much but she was a little immature and young; he knew that also.

'I your girlfriend. You look girl.' Her face turned dark as if a shadow had passed over it.

'What girl?' Dan smiled. That was a few months ago when he still thought it was cute that she was jealous. He knew now that possessive girls in Thailand are no joking matter.

Noi poured herself another Sang Som and soda. 'Girl next table, you look her.' Noi scowled. He had a hard time remembering if there had been a girl seated next to them or not. Had he really looked at her? It didn't matter now anyway.

He had been traveling around the world with his American girlfriend. They had been to many countries including Vietnam, Nepal and India. They had never visited Thailand and planned to stay for a few months. They had been away from home for about a year and his girlfriend wanted to fly home for a few weeks and visit her folks. When the two weeks were almost up, Dan called her and gave her the bad news. He needed time to be on his own and she should not come back. He felt terrible, especially since that was not the real reason. He had met someone else. Damn. Why did she have to go home and leave me alone in Thailand, of all places? She should have left me in India. Everything would have been all right then.

He could hear Noi on her cell phone; her voice sounded strangely far away. The room turned slowly. Dan blinked his eyes and tried to concentrate. She was so beautiful, only twenty-two years old when they'd met. He'd been having a drink one night in Thermae, in Bangkok. She'd told him that she'd been working as a waitress but had just lost her job because she'd protested when a customer had patted her on her rear end. She'd wandered into Thermae by accident and hardly ever came to Sukhumvit Road. Dan had bought her a drink and taken her back to his hotel.

She would appear at odd moments when he went out, and one time she got into his hotel room and hid in the closet. Thank God he had not taken a girl home that night. Maybe it would have been better if he had, then he might have realized ...

He wasn't aware at that time that she was stalking him. Why would she do that when girls at home hardly paid any attention to him? He'd never given it a thought until now—now he was looking at things from another perspective. If I could only go back in time to last year, to see things differently, he thought. If I had only listened to Frank. He told me not to get involved right from the start. Frank had done everything but smack him in the face and he still hadn't got it.

'Listen, did you fall for that bullshit lost-my-good-girl-waitress job? You met her in Thermae, you idiot. What did you think she was doing there, looking for an Ice Cream Sunday or a Big Mac? Thai girls pick up *farang* guys there all the time for cold cash—and speaking of cold, their hearts are the same temperature.' Dan could feel that his shirt was soaked now.

'I love *you*. The girl on the back of my Honda was the girl that works in the grocery store. I was only giving her a lift home. I would never go out with anyone else. You did call, didn't you?'

'What business you I call?' Noi sat next to him on the floor and lit a cigarette. Dan touched his chest. His hand came away sticky and wet.

'Don't worry, it was an accident. You won't get into trouble.'

'No accident and I no worry.' Noi stood up.

'Where are you going? The ambulance should be coming any minute now.'

'Why you speak crazy?' Noi took a flat pink container from her purse.

'The ambulance. You did call an ambulance, didn't you?' Dan could imagine Noi's face screwed up in a scowl, getting darker by the second. Noi opened her compact and checked her make-up in the small mirror.

'I call my girlfriend. We go disco.'

'Call an ambulance. I'm going to die if you don't. I bought you the house in Isaan like you wanted. You said you loved me.'

'Next time you not go with girl.' Noi carefully stubbed the cigarette out in the ashtray. Dan tried to get up but couldn't. He touched the handle of the knife in his chest and strained to lift his head. Everything was becoming blurry. He heard Noi's high heels clicking on the floor, then the door slammed behind her.

The Endless Summer

Rick was having a drink at his favorite bar in Rawai when he heard a loud rumbling getting closer and closer. There was no need for him to turn around; the noise came right up behind him. With a final roar the huge motorcycle came to an abrupt halt. A hand clapped Rick on the back and a voice called for a Sang Som and soda before he received a warm greeting and a hug from his pal Mac. Rick wondered aloud where Mac's latest girl was.

'Took her back,' came the matter-of-fact reply.

'Why? I thought that you really like her.'

'I did, but time's up.'

'Time's up? How long was it? Three days or four?'

'Doesn't matter—when it's time, it's time.'

'Anyone ever tell you that you have a serious problem with intimacy?'

'Not since I left America. Had a girl back there who kept mentioning the dreaded ten-letter C word.'

'Which is?'

'Commitment. One even had the audacity to suggest that I see a psychotherapist, work out my problems. Me! Can you imagine that?'

'I can't for the life of me understand why anyone would suggest that to you.' Rick laughed.

Mac ordered another drink and one more for Rick. 'You know it's so surreal here most of the time. It's like being in a movie. Maybe life is like that—like the movies. Sometimes we're in a comedy and sometimes an adventure film or even a musical.'

'Okay, what movie do you think you are in now?' Rick looked

a bit dubious.

'Do you remember *The Endless Summer*? It was a documentary, shot in beautiful color. Three kids traveled around the world looking for the perfect wave. Well, Thailand is my endless summer—only instead of looking for a tight curl or a long roll, it's tight buns and long legs and there are always a few more just around the bend.'

'Very philosophical.' Rick shook his head.

'Sure it's easy to see. It's summer here all year around.' If Mac was aware of his friend's hesitation he didn't show it and continued on enthusiastically. 'Ponce de León went in the wrong direction. Florida is filled with old people now, America's graveyard. Just think if he had come to Siam instead. Do you realize that I will never grow old here? Can you imagine that?' Mac's grin spread across his entire face.

Rick raised his hand. '*Check bin khap.*' Time to get out of here, he thought.

'No wait. Don't go. Can you comprehend that when I'm seventy, going on seventeen, I will still be going out with twenty-two-year-old girls and riding around on my Harley.'

'Until you drop dead that is, no doubt with a glass of Sang Som in your hand. Do you realize that you sound very shallow?' Rick frowned.

'So be it. I'm not vain or bashful. I admit it. Selfish and shallow is what a woman called me back home and she may have been right.'

'Only one woman called you that?'

'She was a nice lady, others called me much worse. That's one of the reasons that I feel so comfortable here. Like most of the Thais, my long-range plans are terribly short-sighted, except that I recognize the fact.'

Rick jumped up from his stool. 'Do you also recognize the fact that you sound childish and silly? Don't you think you should act your age?'

'There, you've hit it on the head. That's why we're here. We don't have to act our age. What would you have me do, date sixty-year-old women?'

'Might be safer for you. Remember, I was at the restaurant two weeks ago when your girl jumped you, climbed all over you like a fly on rice. Almost knocked your brains out with a beer bottle. Good thing I grabbed her arm in time.'

'Yeah, thanks. That was some night. What was her name again anyway?'

'See, that's exactly what I mean. You can't even remember their names.'

'Sure I can. You know that there are only ten or eleven Thai girls' names in all, don't you?'

Rick left a tip and shoved his change in his pocket. 'How do you figure?'

'Hell, they're all named Lek, Nui, Noi, Oi, Poi, Nuit, Nit.' Mac held his hands out, palms up and nodded his head in a you-know-I'm-right gesture.

'I have to get back to my house, write down all these words of wisdom. Going to make a good short story one day. Any other profound observations?'

'As a matter of fact, yes. Ever notice that when we go into a local bar the girls hardly ever look our way?'

'That's because they know you're a hopeless case.'

'Exactly.' Mac stabbed the air with his finger.

'I was only kidding—well, kind of kidding.'

'But that's it. I've been here five years, understand a bit of the language, am retired and am never going back to the States. That's precisely what they don't want to hear. So now when I go to a new bar and get asked the usual three questions: Where you from? How long you stay here? What you do? I tell them that I just arrive a few days ago, have a very important job and will most certainly return to America.'

'Why?'

'To give them hope, of course. They all either want to leave the country with you or want you to leave by yourself and then have you send them money. And if you can't understand what they say, they can talk about you in front of your face, call you a big-nosed *kee nok*—bird doo-doo. I figure that if they can fib to me I can fib right back.'

'What? Thai bargirls fib?' Rick smiled.

'I'm serious now, and please listen to me as this should be imprinted on everyone's visa: they tell you what you want to hear, and it sounds good, so you believe it. They should print that along with: it's okay to play if you know the rules.'

'Thanks, and let me know when your lonely hearts advice column or book comes out.' Rick sprang for his Honda dream.

'Hey,' Mac shouted with his hand to his mouth, 'many a true word is often spoken in jest.'

No Raving Beauty

When I see a *farang* man walking hand in hand with a homely Thai woman I often wonder, why doesn't this guy have a better-looking companion?' There are plenty of cute ones around. I could practically close my eyes and bump into a better-looking sweetheart than the ones these guys have.

As I became more curious and observant I continually saw couples like this in my neighborhood. The more I looked, the more couples I saw. Most of the men were in their late fifties, sixties or even seventies, while the women all appeared to be fifty years or older and each had that dark skin and sturdy build of a bricklayer or truck driver, typical of the women of Isaan. Not to be unkind, but many had faces that would stop a clock.

I wanted to make friends with some of these people and find out how long they had been together. Possibly some of the women had been attractive when they were younger but from the looks of them, I doubted it. I did meet some of these couples and casually asked how long they had been partners. Most had been with each other for only a few months or a few years. I became more intrigued and naturally the next question I wanted to ask the man was: 'Why don't you have a better-looking companion?' But I couldn't very well say that, could I? I was happy to discover that two of my close friends had not-so-attractive women living with them. Actually one was downright brutal-looking. Even more fortuitous was the fact that the three of us planned on going to Cambodia for a week of sightseeing. This was a perfect opportunity for me to find the answer to my question, if I could find a way to phrase it properly.

As soon as we landed in Phnom Penh we headed straight

for the Le Cyrcee Club. It was a place where the girls were not bashful. We sat at the bar and ordered three gin and tonics. In a matter of seconds a group of girls came over and my friend Reiner declared that this one girl was the most beautiful girl that he had ever seen and started to make arrangements to keep her for the whole week.

Well, from the look of his girl in Thailand I could believe it. Is this how it happens, I thought, by sheer accident? An ugly woman walked up to him in Thailand, by chance, and he fell for her? I begged him, since we had been in Cambodia for all of an hour, not to be so hasty and to walk down the road with me to Sharky's Bar.

It is quite a nice place, on the second floor, with a balcony overlooking the street. It has a few pool tables and a large oval bar with plenty of space to stroll around, and the food is excellent. The big draw is, of course, the girls. Freelancers abound and proliferate as the night goes on. The girls are both Cambodian and Vietnamese. Most are pros but some have regular day jobs and are just looking to pick up a few extra bucks. For my money the girls, especially the Cambodians, are much nicer than the demimondaines in Thailand. They are more friendly and less mercenary.

In Sharky's Bar, the Khmers and the Vietnamese don't hang out with each other. Live and let live. Sometimes as many as a dozen Viet girls arrive with their own mama-san. This is very helpful when they don't speak English. You can make all of the arrangements with the chaperone.

The three of us sat down on the balcony and were immediately surrounded by a dozen Vietnamese beauties. Heaven, this is pure heaven, I thought as three girls wrapped themselves around me. I looked over at Reiner, a big guy from Finland. He had his huge arms around six or seven girls and had a giant grin on his face. I glanced at Nigel from England. He was in a deep conversation with the mama-san. Those of you who have been to Sharky's Bar know that most of the minders are all of an indeterminate age and look like Komodo dragons. Yes, you guessed it. Nigel took the woman back to his room. Why would he choose the oldest and least attractive woman in the place? My two friends had the time of their lives for the week and always came home later than myself. When they came downstairs for breakfast, all of their girls were invariably homely.

'Jeez, if you guys had picked the girls earlier in the evening they wouldn't have been so bad-looking,' I said. They looked at me puzzled.

'What do you mean?'

What's going on? I have to get to the bottom of this, I thought.

The next night, after I'd had more than a few drinks, I asked Nigel why he didn't choose prettier girls as he had many chances, and why he didn't have a younger woman living with him back in Thailand.

'Because the older ones are so grateful,' he said to me with a big smile on his face. Well, I gave up. Was he kidding me? Maybe I would never know why guys here went out with less than attractive girls.

Back in Thailand I decided that I needed a full-time, live-in, all-round housekeeper and girl. The first one I chose was a real cutie pie from a bar in Karon. She cleaned the house a bit and spent the rest of the day watching television. I got rid of her and asked my friend Marc, who has been here a while and speaks Thai, to find me a girl. She was cute too and did a whirlwind job cleaning the house.

One evening at eight o'clock she jumped on her motorbike.

'Where are you going?' I asked.

'I have job in Karaoke. I come back later.'

'You didn't tell me that.'

'I just got job today.'

'Wait. Take all of your clothes with you.'

The problem with hiring a young cutie pie is that they are always trying to find a way to finagle a few more thousand baht, mostly by doing short time at the drop of a hat and with your friends too, if they can.

I took the precaution of showing the next candidate around the house. An adorable twenty year old. I asked if she liked dogs—the whole bit. Okay, she moved in the next day. That night she put my dogs outside.

'What are you doing?'

'Dogs should sleep outside. I no like sleep with dogs.'

I took her and showed her the couch on the front porch. 'You no like sleep with dog. You sleep here. Dogs sleep inside.'

That was the end of her.

I was getting discouraged trying to find a live-in and called an old girlfriend of mine.

'Meet me at the café down the street. Lots of girls go there and I can translate for you,' she said. I spoke to the owner of the cafe and told her that I was looking for a live-in housekeeper and girlfriend. I offered her a 1,000-baht reward and, by george, in two days she brought me a girl right off the bus from Roi-Et. Twenty-two years old, no babies, no tattoos, no English and sturdily built. She told me that in three months she had to go back home for a week and help her parents with the harvest.

'What did you do before?' I inquired.

'I farmer.' And I believed her as she sure looked the part.

Okay, she moved in and is doing a great job. Cleans the house from top to bottom every day, makes me breakfast and feeds the three dogs and the one cat.

Saa goes shopping at the outdoor market, buys and cooks the chicken and fish for the animals. I can send her into the supermarket by herself. She makes me frozen fruit drinks and waits on me hand and foot. The bottom line for me was always, 'Would I bar fine this girl out?' And I have to say no, I would not pay a bar fine for Saa.

And I am not really very interested in having sex with her.

On the other hand I am very happy with her. She in turn is very happy and grateful to be here.

I found the answer to my conundrum easily and by accident. Now I understand.

Sounds Good to Me

There's more than one reason why we fall in love so soon after coming to Thailand. The girls are beautiful with hard bodies, great figures and are charming. They are young, available, ready and willing. What's not to like?

The girls in America are also attractive and accessible. However, they know what they want and are not bashful about asking for it. More likely than not, they tell you what's on their minds right away and what they expect from you. One girl that I went out with only twice asked me if I wanted to get married.

'What?' I laughed. 'Are you proposing to me on our second date?'

'No. But if you don't want to get married, let me know now so I don't waste my time going out with you.'

'How would I know, since I don't even have a girlfriend.'

'Just tell me. In the future, sometime, would you get married?'

'Jeez, this is an important decision. Can I think it over for a while?'

A typical man–woman conversation in America.

The girls in Thailand—most never making it past grade school—are still smarter than the girls back home. Thai girls figure out what you want first. They know what they want but let it rest until they think you are in a suitable state of euphoria. Which leads me to another great quote by my friend Jake in Cambodia: they tell you what you want to hear, it sounds good, so you believe it.

Heck, it's not hard to figure out what a man wants and it's easy to offer it to him. Sweet words, no matter how far-fetched they may seem, play a big part in the start of a relationship in Thailand. We have all walked past bars and heard 'handsome man come here' called out to us. Now, even though we know that they are seeking the 1,000-baht bills in our wallet, we must admit that it is a bit thrilling to have all these beauties available and inviting us to sample their charms.

Most of the Thai girls or bargirls that I go out with start by putting their arms around me saying, 'I like you,' looking me right in the eye or resting their head on my chest. Well, I think to myself, that sounds reasonable enough.

In the case of an older guy like me the next thing that comes is: 'I don't like young man, he butterfly, drink too much, go out too much.' Then, putting a small soft hand on my chest, she says, 'You *jai dee*. You have good heart. You take care me. I like you too much.' This is pretty flattering coming from a twenty-two-year-old beauty.

They tell you what you want to hear and you have to admit that it does sound pretty good. I have always been saved by the reality of looking in the mirror at night before I go to bed. Nope, my face has not miraculously changed into a double for Brad Pitt. These girls are so charming and sound so sincere that if they kept it up they will have Boris Karloff thinking that he is Cary Grant. So you can't blame guys for falling in love here—purchasing bars, buffalos, and houses for their significant others.

As for me, I just keep in mind Jake's words of wisdom: they tell you what you want to hear, it sounds good, so you believe it.

Sometimes when they tell you what they think you want to hear they don't always get it right. But they're like the Energizer Bunny or the Timex watch advertisements—they just keep on ticking. My ex-girlfriend Soopies told me that she wanted to live with me for a year, then get married, then after a year we would have children. It sounded all so very sensible and realistic.

However, I dislike kids. I certainly don't want to have any and I much prefer to live with my two dogs. When I turned down what seemed like a great offer, Soopies was surprised, then baffled, then angry.

She had wasted months of her good time softening me up.

She continued to speak gently, not giving in just yet. 'We can start living together right now. I want to sleep with you every night, wake up with you every morning.' Her arms were around me and her moist lips brushed my ear as she spoke. It sounded tempting, very tempting indeed, I have to admit. But I was waiting for the other shoe to drop.

'We can buy a house together, move right in.'

Sure, I knew it. For a Thai girl 'buying a house together' means me paying for it and her having it in her name. Soopies was not finished yet. Sometimes they have the adroitness to tell you what they think you don't want to hear.

A few weeks later she came over my house to give me the next installment.

'My darling. I have something very sad to tell you. I am almost out of money and I must work to support my mother and daughter. The only way I can make enough money is to work in a bar in Patong. Please don't be mad at me if you see me there. I must start this week.' I knew for sure that Soopies thought too highly of herself to work in a mere bar. What? Her, stand around at a bar all night like goods on a shelf? No way that would happen. I also knew that she was freelancing at the VIP Club across the street from Soi Bangla. She was asking for and receiving 5,000 baht per evening. Soopies was the last girl that I would be worried about making a living. She expected me to jump up, throw my arms in the air and shout, 'No, No, anything but that! Don't work in a bar. How much money do you need to stay home?'

The best reply I could muster was, 'Really?' Once again she was annoyed as hell.

I went to Cambodia with a buddy, Fat Larry, who, for a guy from New York, is incredibly naive. We picked up a couple of hookers in Sharky's Bar. The next day, over breakfast, Larry told me, 'You know that my girl graduated from the university and is qualified to be an architect.'

'What? Are you stupid or something?' I asked.

'It's true. Her father passed away just as she was in her final semester and she was forced to become a prostitute to pay her fathers debts and to support the family.'

'Wake up and smell the coffee, you moron.'

'Listen, Frank. I know she's telling me the truth because she speaks such perfect English.'

'And do you know how she learned to speak English so well?' I leaned closer to him, raising my voice.

'From f—king 4,000 *farang*s, that's how!'

Now, do you think that Larry believed me or her? Her, of course. It's Jake's theory: they tell you what you want to hear, it sounds good, so you believe it.

And to this day Fat Larry swears that every word of her story is true.

I received a phone call from my friend Gerald who has retired in Thailand from America. He is selling time shares in Patong, working six days a week, commission only but it is low season so no luck. His pension is not all that big and he could use a few extra bucks. He has been casting around for a small business. I told him that opening a business entailed spending a good deal of money to incorporate and obtain a work permit and pay taxes. He just called today to tell me he had it all solved. He has been dating a very nice Thai girl who offered to help him.

Her plan is to open up a small tourist and travel stand. She will have all the paperwork done, open the stand and work in it. All he has to do is put up 50,000 baht, then sit around and collect the money when it comes in.

'Sounds great,' Gerald said.

You know what I told him, don't you.

Why Do They Do It?

I often wonder what makes a guy go totally off the deep end when he meets a cute young Thai girl. A psychologist explained it very well when he said falling in love is a form of madness. So true.

Hell, it happened to me back home in America when I was young. I was totally gaga, blindly in love. There's nothing as exciting as that first brush with heart-filling, mind-numbing love. It happened to me a few times and I feel so lucky to have had that experience.

Older and wiser now, (a lot older) having lived in New York City for the past twenty years and having my balls broken and my heart too by the best the city has to offer, I feel fairly confident here in Phuket. When a lithe young thing wraps herself around me and the smell of jasmine starts seeping into my brain, I simply get up and look in the mirror. What do I see? Forty miles of bad road that's rough enough to wake anyone up, and this nineteen-year-old beauty laying next to me is declaring her undying love and mentioning the purchase of a house at the same time. I really have to laugh to myself at that. But the girls just say what they think you want to hear. However this has been covered in my previous chapters.

What I really want to write about is: why do so many people come here and open businesses? I figure that there are three groups: guys buying bars for their girls, Westerners and couples opening stores, and competent business people who know what they are doing and have planned ahead. We will not waste time on these people. They're okay—like my friend Richard. He came here three years ago and opened a real estate business. Didn't have to invest a lot—worked hard and long and is doing well now. God bless him.

Let's talk about the first group.

I met Emile at Don's Restaurant in Rawai. He claimed that he had not slept with his wife in seventeen years and that they lived in opposite ends of the house. We went out for a drink to a girly bar. He was not quite sure how to relate and was a bit uneasy. I have to keep an eye on this guy, I thought, because when he falls it's going to be hard. He moved to Isaan where it was cheaper to live. I eventually received a note from him saying he'd found a bargirl who was different. His exact words were that he felt 'like a beautiful flower with all the girls buzzing around him'. Jeez, you can't make this stuff up. He was opening a bar and did I want to visit him. I knew right there and then that it was too late to help him. I should have given him more advice, possibly some books to read. I doubt that it would have helped though.

The problem is that most of these guys have not been out with an attractive girl in the past forty years and possibly never.

'But still he teetered and stumbled under the anaesthesia of her attentions. A Thai female could stand right in front of me and tell me in detail all of the terrible things she is going to do to me and it wouldn't matter. As soon as she puts her hand on my arm I'm dead meat.'

Mm, that sounds familiar, I wonder who said that—but it's true isn't it?

My Canadian lawyer who works with a Thai law firm says that part of the problem is that a guy sells a house back home and the house he bought for US$35,000 twenty-five years ago now sells for US$600,000. That plus his pension or retirement fund and he's on easy street. What's a measly ten grand for a bar when you have this hot little honey breathing down your neck? This is a good theory and it may be true, but not in Emile's case; he was just scraping by.

Another friend, a Norwegian man, bought an open-air bar in

Karon, where the U-shaped driveway is with all the bars.

He named it The Viking's Boat and was so happy he could hardly contain himself. They nabbed him for a million baht for little more than an open-air bar, a few stools and a refrigerator and he still had to pay rent—but hey, his girlfriend wanted it. He rented a house for 25,000 baht a month and bought a big Honda bike. He was living large.

After a few months he had to sell the bike to pay the rent and in a few more months he had to go back home to work. Possibly, as the psychologist inferred, 'These guys are simply nuts.'

What I really find interesting is when middle-aged couples come here on vacation and immediately decide that they want to stay here and open a business. Don't they have better sense? But I suppose a form of romantic madness sets in.

A very nice French couple opened a small restaurant a few blocks away from me. I went with some friends and had French beef stew, which was merely passable taste-wise. It was a small portion and priced at 100 baht more than it should have been. I pass this restaurant often and they never have any customers. Why do they do it? How can they stay open?

The *Phuket Gazette* was very kind and gave them a half-page review, nicely done. I was tempted to write a letter to the editor to say if anyone wanted French food they had better hurry on down. I didn't have the heart.

I was thinking of sending in a list of questions for prospective business people to the *Phuket Gazette*. I sure don't have all the answers but I do have a bunch of questions; it is way too late for these people. I learned from that review. In the interview the couple stated: they had come to Phuket and loved it; they wanted to stay here; they once had a business of some kind back home in a foreign country.

That was the full extent of their thoughts and planning. Duh. Would it not behoove a prospective entrepreneur to think along the lines of:

1. Is there a need for this type of business? (There are forty food stands and all types of restaurants within shouting distance of the French restaurant.)
2. Exactly why would anyone set foot inside my store?
3. Do I know what my start-up costs will be?
4. And monthly operating costs?
5. What is my daily or monthly break-even point?
6. How many customers will I need to come in every day and how much will they have to spend in order for me to break even?

Sadly the French restaurant closed before they could find out. But hope springs eternal and they have re-opened a block down the street in a beautiful store three times the size with plenty of parking and a higher rent to match. They thought that they would do better in a higher-profile establishment and they still don't have any business.

Listen, dear friends. Don't even think of opening a business unless you have a very good answer for each of the above six questions.

I can only think that visitors and couples can fall madly in love with the beauty of this island, go insane and lose their powers of reason.

Bargirlish

I went to the bookstore the other day and noticed all the helpful books about Thailand—Thai–English dictionaries, *Culture Shock! Thailand*, *How To Do Business in Thailand*, *Love, Sex and Trust in Thailand*—and I got to thinking that what we really need is an English translation of the sentences bargirls utter. Now if we only knew what they really meant.

Lady: 'You handsome man you.'
Translation: 'Handsome for a big-nosed, fat, ugly *farang*.'

Lady: 'I come work bar two days only.'
Translation: 'Five years in this crummy dump, night in, night out, and they still ask me the same stupid questions.'

Lady: 'You live where?'
Translation: 'How much can I ask this guy for if he is staying at an expensive hotel?'

Lady: 'You come from where?'
Translation: 'Please God, not another cheapskate Italian.'

Lady: 'I love you too much.'
Translation: 'I love your wallet too much.'

Lady: 'It is my birthday tomorrow.'
Translation: 'This is the 127th birthday that I have had this year and can we go to the gold shop tomorrow?'

Lady: 'Oh, you sexy man, I help you make good boom-boom.'
Translation. 'Let's get this over with so I can go back to the bar.'

Lady: 'I never go with *farang* before.'
Translation: 'Well, not in the past half an hour anyway.'

Lady: 'I no like work bar. I want to finish bar.'
Translation: 'Can you send me money every month along with the three other morons.'

Lady: 'Up to you.' (smiling demurely)
Translation: 'For now, but you will pay later, for sure.'

Lady: 'I love you, want to come to America with you.'
Translation: 'I'd go to Transylvania with Dracula to get out of here.'

Lady: 'I make you good wife, cook and clean every day for you, take care of you when you get old.'
Translation: 'Unless I find a man with more money.'

Lady: 'I so afraid: to stay alone, of your large organ, etc.'
Translation: 'Yeah, like a tiger in a hen house.'

Lady: 'I cannot. I too shy.'
Translation: 'Cough up some more cash, buddy.'

Lady: 'Can you drive me to Robinson's?'
Translation: 'Let's see how many outfits I can get this guy to spring for.'

Lady: 'This is my brother.'
Translation: 'This is my Thai boyfriend.'

Lady: 'Drink for me, please?'
Translation: 'Thirty-baht commission for me, please?'

Lady: 'Thank you for the drink. Excuse me for a minute while I speak to my girlfriend.'
Translation: 'I want to make the rounds and see how many other jerks I can get to buy me a drink.'

Lady: 'I meet you at eight o'clock tomorrow.'
Translation: 'Or nine or ten, if I even show up at all.'

Lady: 'My mother very sick, need operation, have no money.'
Translation: 'Hey, I know that this is the oldest line in the book but you know what? It works sometimes.'

Lady: 'Yes, I can give you very good smoke.'
Translation: 'If you like Marlboros, that is.'

Lady: 'I no work bar, only stop here for drink. I good girl.'
Translation: 'Of course I work here, you idiot.'

Lady: 'I no butterfly girl.'
Translation: 'Helicopter would be more like it.'

Lady: 'I want to eat seafood, very healthy.'
Translation: 'I want to eat seafood, very expensive.'

Lady: 'Can I use your phone? It's a local call.'
Translation: 'It's a local call if you live in Hamburg.'

Lady: 'I love you, want you to meet Mama and Poppa.'
Translation: 'I want a free all-expenses-paid trip to Khon Kaen and bring some extra cash as my parents will need some things also.'

Lady: 'Hello, how are you?'
Translation: 'Hello, how is your wallet?'

Lady: 'I love so much. Can I see you tomorrow?'
Translation: 'I need to make some money here.'

Lady: 'Can you loan me 3,000 baht? I will pay you back during the week.'
Translation: 'I'm leaving tomorrow.'

Lady: 'I no lie to you, always tell truth.'
Translation: 'I always lie—about everything. What does it mean, truth?'

Lady: 'My mother is very sick and I must go home to take care of her for two weeks.'
Translation: 'The German guy that has been sending me money every month is coming and it's imperative that I stay with him.'

It's a Great Life

L ek stood near the front of the open-air bar on Soi Sea Dragon watching the tourists stroll by. At a distance she could easily tell the difference between a tourist and a local. The tourists were usually wide-eyed, like people staring up at the tall buildings on a visit to New York City. They also dressed a lot better. She knew they had plenty of money in their pockets—'expendable cash' was the term a *farang* friend had used.

Her job was to get them to come in and spend it. She ignored anyone that looked as if they had been there a while, unless she thought that they had promise—unless she could see the longing in their eyes, the complete fascination when they looked at her. In those cases she considered taking it further as she wasn't interested in making a few thousand baht every night, not interested at all.

Lek didn't shout: 'Handsome man, come here, welcome!' That was ridiculous, old hat. She merely waited until she made eye contact with a man, then she would point to him then to a seat, as though she was ordering him in. It surprised them. They were even more surprised when she broke into a self-deprecating grin and shrugged her shoulders as if they had just shared a joke together, nodding her head in the direction of the bar. They usually filed in like captivated schoolkids.

She was a 'front' and she was excellent at it. She was paid more money than all of the other girls put together, but she wasn't impressed by that fact. She had bigger fish to fry. The other girls caged drinks from the customers—forty-baht commission for a Malibu and orange juice that cost 140 baht—then tried to talk the client into taking them home. Short time was the ideal for them. Four-hundred-baht bar fine, of which they got half, then

2,000 for taking off their clothes and having sex. It didn't matter what the man looked like: fat and sweaty, bald, tall and skinny or hairy (that was the absolute worst). They closed their eyes and let it happen, and when it was over they made a fast 2,200 baht, not counting a few drink commissions.

Small money, Lek thought, smiling, hardly worth bothering with. That's the problem with these people, hicks from the sticks, mostly Isaan rice planters. They come here and think they've hit the big time—they have no idea.

Lek was one of the most beautiful girls in Phuket, possibly *the* most beautiful and easily the most charming. She had flowing red hair, large full breasts and long legs. She didn't wear revealing clothes, she didn't have too, and besides, that was not part of her persona. Lek kept herself above the bar scene; she was there but not part of it. The men walking by—if they had any sense at all and were not bleary-eyed with beer—noticed this right away. Most men, as corny as they knew it sounded, could not help but think and most times would actually say, 'What's a nice girl like you doing in a place like this?'

Lek had two stock answers: 'A girl's got to make a living,' she would reply with a big carefree smile. That was the answer she most often gave. But if she sensed something more in the question she would sigh and speak quietly, almost whispering, 'not good for me,' with a sad look of resignation on her face. She held that answer back, saving it for a special person not some fat-bellied German, some jerk in shorts and a T-shirt or your usual tourist. No, the man that she said that to had to have something on the ball. He would be smarter than the average guy; he would be better dressed than the rest of them—no fake Rolex for him. For Christ's sake, she had seen thousands of the damn things.

If she was pressed by a man to have a drink with him, she would. She would never ever, under any circumstances, ask for one. She would thank him gratefully for the drink then look into his eyes and hesitate, as if she wanted to share a secret. She would smile and keep silent. After a while, if he kept asking, she would shake her head and say, 'I'm so tired of this, night after night, but what can I do? I need to eat. I need a job. I need to send money to my parents.'

She wouldn't look up at the man she was talking to; she didn't have to. She had the timing down; she had it just right. She could hear his mind whirling, clicking like some crazed pinball machine. She was in no hurry: if it happens, it happens. You can't rush these things, she thought. They had to suggest it themselves. She would never say it, never. If she was patient—and she was—the man would always ask, 'Can I help you?'

Of course, they had other things on their minds; she expected that, accepted it, welcomed it. 'There's nothing you can do,' she would reply. 'If I only had my own place, not a bar but a restaurant, a nice place, where decent people came, I would be happy—but I have nothing. I send all of the money I make—and it's not much—home to my mother.'

The previous month Lek took a man for a million baht. She made love to him, reluctantly at first, then with more passion until he was crazed with the very being of her. 'I have to go back to the bar. I need to make money. I wish I did not have to go.'

It was so easy. He just went to the bank and handed her a million baht. 'Now you can have a restaurant. Now you and I can stay together.' She never opened the restaurant; she just put the money in the bank and laughed at the silliness of it all. She called the police and had him taken away when he complained.

Lek felt satisfied with her life. She did not have to take any man home. She owned three houses: two here in Phuket and one in Nakhon Si Thammarat. She was completely independent and would retire in a few more years at the tender age of twenty-seven. She noticed, out of the corner of her eye, a man that looked familiar walking towards her. 'Excuse me,' she said to her present client, and rose to greet the man that was coming closer, walking purposefully.

She recognized him. It was a man that had loved her for two months the year before. She had only taken him for 80,000 baht. How important could this be, she thought?

'I have to talk to you. I love you. Come back with me. I need you.' The man's face was flushed and red. He was shaking. 'I can't live without you.'

Lek had heard all this before. It was just part of the job. 'Up to you,' she smiled.

The man yanked a pistol from his pocket and pushed the muzzle against her breast. He pulled the trigger and she flew back against the bar. In the next second, before anyone could stop him, he put the pistol to his temple.

A New Twist

It was about ten in the evening at the Happy Bar in Karon. No one looked especially happy. It was off-season, the tourists were gone and the bargirls watched TV, slumped in their seats. Peter finished his drink and toyed with the idea of taking a girl home. But all of the pretty ones had gone; they'd already made enough money to sit out the coming months in comfort. Most had gone back to their villages and parent's homes in Isaan.

Peter paid his check and pushed himself up from the bar. His car was parked across the street. He walked past the booths set up in the parking lot. They were selling clothes, sunglasses, watches and the usual tourist souvenirs. Then he saw her—a stunning girl wearing a short blouse and hip-hugger pants exposing a bare, flat waist. She was the most beautiful girl that he had ever seen.

Peter started talking to her and asked if he could buy her a drink. The girl, called Nok, accepted the invitation. She spoke English very well and smiled constantly. He thought that she was charming. He learned that she was nineteen years old and lived here in Phuket with her sister, Neung, having just come up from Nakhon Si Thammarat. They ended up going to his house together and making love. It was wonderful. She sat close to him on the drive back and he pressed a 1,000-baht bill into her hand.

'What's this? What am I, a bargirl?' Nok was furious. 'I've never made love before on a first date but I did with you because I really liked you. And now you think I'm a whore.' She burst into tears and thrust the bill back at him without even looking at it.

Peter apologized profusely for his mistake. It had been so long since he had been out with a normal girl that he'd forgotten how to act. The apologies seemed to work, and after that he saw her every day. They spent the afternoons at Nai Harn Beach. She wore a bikini and they played in the waves. Those were some of the best days that he could remember. He caught many an envious glance from the male tourists sitting on their loungers. They went out for dinner at night then to the clubs for a drink. They danced close together and he was as happy as he had ever been in his entire life. Nok never asked him for a dime.

One night, after a romantic evening, Nok kissed him gently and said that she wanted to become engaged to him. Her plan was not to rush into anything, she said. She loved him deeply and wanted to be with him forever. After a year together they would be married and then in another year they would have children. She wanted a little boy that looked just like him.

Although he had been afraid to admit it, even to himself, Peter had been in love with Nok for some time. He would love to have a daughter with her, and he wanted his baby to look just like Nok. Peter agreed to her suggestion in a heartbeat and they started to make plans to visit her parents in the coming month to make arrangements. He could not remember ever being so amazingly in love.

Nok still lived with her sister, Neung, who worked in a bar in Patong. Neung had been in Phuket for five years and her favorite line for the suckers was that she'd just arrived and had never made love to a *farang* before. She was afraid, she said because she had heard that they were 'veeery big' and she didn't want to be hurt. The customers fell for it every time and when she moaned and cried, they felt quite powerful. She was making a fortune and Nok was a bit envious.

One night at dinner Nok seemed upset and distracted. Peter asked her what was the matter. She said that she loved him and wanted to be completely honest with him. She had met a very wealthy tourist living all by himself on a large sailing boat. It seemed that he was quite smitten by her and had offered her 80,000 baht if she would stay with him on his boat to keep him company for one month.

Nok pointed out that Neung had been sending money home to their parents every month and she herself had no money and could send nothing. This was an opportunity to prove that she was a good daughter. She had decided that she was going to accept the man's offer. She would see Peter as often as she could get away and she hoped that he would understand. He was stunned, speechless. Was this what she really wanted to do?

'I have to have this money. I can not go home empty-handed. I will have no face,' Nok stressed.

'Of course, if you really loved me, you would not let me do this. You have the power to stop me by simply giving me the money that I need.'

Peter hesitated. Eighty thousand baht was a great deal of money to him. He stared at her, silent.

'You gave money to bargirls before. Am I less than a bargirl that you can't give me any money?'

Nok's voice became higher and louder. 'I am less than a whore to you? That's what I am? Lower than a whore?'

Nok was screaming and crying now. 'We are supposed to see my parents and become engaged and now this is stopping us. I love you so much but you are forcing me to turn into a whore like my sister. Why can't you help me?' Nok sobbed with her head down.

He could hardly afford it but he went to the bank and withdrew 80,000 baht and gave it to Nok. It was agreed that they would go to see her parents at the beginning of the week. Peter was sure that he had done the right thing; it was all worth it.

He did not see Nok the following day or the day after that. She did not answer her cell phone. He couldn't find her and was worried about her. He went to see her sister, Neung, in Patong. Peter knocked on the door of her apartment. Neung was half-asleep and looked surprised and almost annoyed to see him. 'Why is everyone looking for my sister? There was a Canadian guy here from the Boat Lagoon early this morning. He said something about giving her 80,000 baht—and now you. Didn't she tell you? She went to Holland yesterday with a scuba instructor.'

A Tribute to
the Girls of Thailand

I was thinking the other day that as much as I complain, rant and rave about dealing with Thai girls, I am still a lot better off here than in America. Having been here eight years I kind of forgot what the dating and marriage scene was like back home.

My friend said that some Thai girls want you to buy a buffalo for their parents and the rest are looking to marry a beast of burden. That lit a bulb in my head. I had almost forgotten my ex-wife in America. After we'd got married I felt that I was just a stepping stone for her, or rather a donkey used by her to get from one place to another. I believe that she married me to get out of her house after college. Her parents were unpleasant, and strict Italian Catholics to boot. There would be no living together for us without the benefit of holy matrimony. In the late 1950s and early 1960s, marriage was the only way. Having graduated from high school in the late 1950s, we were all comfortable with this concept. It was the times that we were living in.

The songs on the radio in those days were 'When We Get Married', 'My Eyes Adored You', and so on. These were true romantic love songs only to be replaced a few years later by songs such as 'Lay Upon My Big Brass Bed'. Christ, don't even think about the stupid sex rap songs the kids listen to now.

One may complain about Thai girls lying and cheating and taking possession of the house but that's a slap on the wrist compared to getting divorced in America. I loved my wife with all of my heart—as men do Thai girls here—and I thought and

91

expected that we would be together for the rest of our lives. A few years after we were married she started having sex with more than a few guys. Upwardly mobile was the way she thought of herself. If I had known her longer I might have seen how completely self-absorbed she was, how self-concerned and selfish. No, I was blindly in love. I bought her a new car and a mink coat. We went to Europe every year and lived the good life. She met a guy that owned half a dozen jewelry stores and, heck, I was only a chef in a restaurant. Chefs in those days were just hard-working stiffs with no prestige, not like today. She figured that her lifestyle was going to improve dramatically, so goodbye Frank and hello the good life.

She was promiscuous and changed men like shoes, much like the girls here. So what's the difference? When something like this happens hearts are broken, no matter what country you are in. The only difference is in the financial cost. Thank God we did not have children. As it was, she left me—and still got a new car, her mink coat, of course, and we divided up all of our furniture and belongings. After we had made a list she said that she really did not want anything and would I like to purchase her half; talk about adding insult to injury. I also had to pay for her lawyer and we split my bank account. And here I was only a few weeks ago complaining that I had to give my Thai girlfriend 16,000 baht to move out. Shame on me. I should have given her a big kiss and a gold chain to boot. Come to think of it now, I had this African–American girl living with me in America for a year. Now they say white people are racist but black people are racist too, even more so, I think. Possibly because they have been getting the short end of the stick for years. I told her she was racist and why was she going out with me because obviously I am white. You know what she said? 'All the black guys with money are either drug dealers or professional businessmen. I don't want to go out with drug dealers and the legally successful black men all want to go out with white blondes. So here I am with you.'

Talk about being brutally honest. I got sick and tired of her crap and guess what? Like the Thai girl that I had she did not want to move out either. 'I need US$2,000 if you want me to go. That's for a month's rent and a month's security'.

Now in America it's difficult to evict anyone. They will sue you at the drop of a hat. Luckily I had a duplex office at the restaurant that I was managing so I said, 'I'm changing the locks in a week and I will not be here. Better get your crap out while you can.' I ended up giving her a hundred bucks for the movers. The mover was a friend of hers and asked me how I felt about her leaving.

I said, 'Today I feel like the guy that bought the sailing boat then sold it.'

Later on I moved to New York City and started dating. Now if you think the girls in Thailand are piranhas, you haven't hit the dating scene in the Big Apple. One thing the girls here and abroad have in common is that if you want a nice girl, you have to get her as soon as she gets off the boat ... er ... bus. A few years in the city or at a girly bar will turn the sweetest little thing into a man-eater.

The nice thing about Thailand is that when you ask a girl where she would like to go she usually says 'Up to you.' Ha! Not so at all in New York. I asked this stunning Haitian girl to have a drink with me and she said, 'Okay, let's meet at the Old King Cole Room.' Jeez, that's in the St. Regis Hotel. There is no place more expensive in New York for drinks than at a hotel. It was our first date and I agreed. Then it seemed that every time Ian Schrager opened a new hotel we had to go there for drinks, or to the River Café or the Rainbow Room over looking the Rockefeller Center. Now a drink is at least twelve bucks and you can't really cheap out and have just one, so you are looking at a minimum of sixty bucks plus tax and tip just for drinks after work. Dinner costs at least US$125 (if you are lucky) and you still have the cab fare to contend with. So when my Thai girlfriend asks for spending money I'm happy to hand over 1,000 baht.

Leave a tip of a dollar or two in New York and you'll be lucky to escape alive. In Thailand you're a big hero if you give a few bucks.

I have to laugh when my lady friends back home say to me, 'What do you have in common with a Thai girl half your age? What can you two possibly talk about?' The answer is nothing, of course, but I always want to go on and tell these *farang* women, 'How about you? What do you talk about? Some inane conversation you had with your hairdresser? Give me a break.'

I can't count the number of nights that I sat having dinner with some *farang* girl while she babbled on about nothing. I'm sitting there waiting for it to be over so I can take her home and make boom-boom. Really, what do we men have in common with women and what do we talk about to each other? Nothing, thats what.

That Haitian girl that I dated? I was crazy about her and was determined to take her to bed no matter how long I had to go out with her. Now three dates is usually the maximum for me. No going home with me in three dates and it's goodbye sweetheart; but in this case I was persistent. I went out with this girl seven times before I got her home. Seven times! Think of the money I expended on all those fancy diners and at clubs like Area, Xenon, Club A, Studio 54. Christ, it must have been US$1,000 easily. In Thailand if you see a beautiful girl, a real knockout, all you have to do is to hold up a few thousand baht and she's yours. No muss, no fuss, no more nonsensical conversations, a done deal without having to make small talk. God, what a pleasure. A shallow view? Okay, you're right. I'm shallow. But ask any man if he disagrees with me.

Are these Thai cultural issues or universal gender issues? I vote for the latter and this is why: the girls in New York are beautiful but tough. Like their Thai counterparts they are on the lookout for big game. They are white hunters, to coin a phrase.

Meet a girl in a bar in New York and for sure she will ask what you do for a living. Of course, they are evaluating your suitability. Are you good enough for them?

Now, I owned a restaurant and was doing okay, or so I thought. But no, not good enough for a beauty there. Investment banker is the only suitable answer. Stock broker? Nah, sorry, not good enough. Vice president? Maybe, if the company is Yahoo.

One girl had the temerity to say to me, 'Where do you see yourself in five years from now?' I said, 'By Christ, I hope it's not in some restaurant talking to stupid girls asking me dumb questions like this.' First dates in America often turn out to be like job interviews.

Back in Thailand watch the girls in the Banana Disco in Phuket, casting an appraising eye over every guy that comes in. You can spot these girls easy. They are at the bar on the left as you walk in and are dressed to the nines, all very attractive. They don't want to go out with me either. What are they looking for? A two-weeker with wide eyes and white shoes, a walking money machine that does not know the score yet. The type of guys *katoey*s scramble over. On his first night here my friend, fat Larry from New York, took a *katoey* home and thought he was with a movie star until his friend gave him the bad news at breakfast.

Most times I think to myself, 'Is it any wonder individuals like me are enamored of Thai women?'

The girls in both countries could eat nails and spit rust but the Thais are so darn charming and sweet that you just don't think of them as being able to stab you to death and then cut you into a rare steak with the same knife—and they can—just like their sisters in America. Thai girls whisper sweet things in your ear, put their arms around you and are always smiling. Who wouldn't be enamored?

The girls in New york are haughty, conceited, snobbish, self-important and are also on the lookout for their own personal ATM—just like here. The difference being that Thai girls are a whole lot sweeter.

After living in America how could you not fall deeply in love here, or at least deeply in like. The deviation between whores in Thailand and whores in America is that here the hookers try to make it a girlfriend experience and are so charming that you really could fall in love. In America when you pay a hooker for sex she couldn't care less if you lived or died.

Thai girls will lie to you at the drop of a hat. They lie about the time of day for no reason. They wouldn't know the truth if it bit them in the rear end, as I have said many times.

'Ouch, what was that?'

'That was the truth, my darling, biting you in the ass.'

'Yes, but what does it mean, the truth? I don't understand. Is there a word in Thai for this?'

But then I stop and think about all of the girls that I dated back home, and it was more than a few what with me owning a very popular restaurant; even if you are a bartender, no matter what you look like, some girls will want to go out with you. I can't think of one of those girls that didn't lied to me at one time or another. So it's the same all over the world. Okay, all you ladies out there, calm down, it's possible that men tell a fib or two also.

I find that the Thai girl's approach to sex as a natural part of life is simply wonderful. Boy, isn't it the truth. All those girls in New York, all the ones that I had living with me, taking them all over the city, to restaurants, nightclubs and Broadway shows, all those gym memberships I paid for, leather pants, gold bracelets— no kidding, it was same as here only more expensive. All that and if I wanted to have sex in the morning or whenever I wanted to it was always a big deal for them, like they were doing me a favor.

In Thailand all I have to do is point to the bed and say boom-boom. Thank you God. What a pleasure.

Just let me mention one more stroke of sagacity: you are prey. Wow, that's great. They should stamp that in your passport on arrival in Thailand, or even when you reach puberty. You are prey!

If more men understood this, the world would be a better place to live in. I will end my latest diatribe with many thanks to the wonderful women of Thailand for reminding me how easy we have it here, in spite of all my complaints.

Amazing Thailand

I had wanted to come to Thailand for quite some time and was looking forward to visiting Andrew, my friend from England who was teaching English at a local language school. He had settled in comfortably with a sweet Thai girl and I was on my way to have dinner with them. I carried written instructions: take the number eleven bus on Sukhumvit Road, pass the Democracy Monument, Khao San Road, then cross over the Phra Pin-klao Bridge. Get off at the second stop and turn left down the first *soi* which, he explained, was a tiny street.

My friend lived in an old building but it did have a security guard, who called my friend before he would let me enter. I took the elevator and found their apartment. Nui greeted me at the door and I removed my shoes. I knew to do that much, at least. I saw that there were four place settings on the bamboo floor mat instead of three. Andrew handed me a drink.

'Sang Thip and soda, good local rum. Nui's girlfriend is coming. You're going to like her. She has a great personality.' Warning bells went off in my head. It sounds like the kiss of death when people say that a girl has 'a good personality'. It really means that the girl is plain-looking or downright ugly. I should have another drink, I thought, or two—even better. The three of us sat down on red cushions where there was quite a spread laid out: a whole fish, crabs, shrimp, salad and rice. Little bowls of condiments such as fish sauce and hot sauce filled every space.

'You really don't want to get involved in that bargirl scene,' said Nui. What a night this was turning out to be. She was starting to sound like my Aunt Helen, who occasionally attempted to fix me up with a date. The girls she chose all invariably looked like people that my Aunt Helen would go out with. I had my back to the door when the bell rang. Andrew opened the door and as I turned slightly, the first thing I saw was a pair of black high heels. Then legs—unbelievably beautiful, long legs. They went all the way up to a black leather miniskirt. Above that was a bare waist as flat and smooth as a tabletop. A white tank top completed the outfit. She had full red lips and long black hair, but it was her stunning smile that did it. I wondered if Colgate knew about her—or the shampoo people. She looked as though if she shook her head, her long hair would float around in slow motion, just like in the TV commercials.

'You must be Frank. I'm Jasmine.'

She looked directly at me and smiled. She was dazzling. Her smile reached out to me, enveloped me, flowed over me, held me captive as sure as if I were in an episode of *Star Trek*. Captain Kirk! Phasers on full power. Zap! I couldn't speak. I stopped breathing.

'Sorry I'm late. You must be hungry. Let's eat.'

Jasmine sat down beside me. Nui made more drinks. The food was delicious. Jasmine peeled a shrimp, leaned over and placed it in my mouth. I could see her cleavage; her breasts were round and full, straining to burst out of their confinement. I couldn't take my eyes off her. She laughed. 'The shrimp is the only thing on the menu tonight.' She smiled at me. It was a confident smile, knowing and wise. This girl could read my mind. I felt I had known her forever.

Dinner flew by. It was time to leave. I walked her to the elevator. She stood close to me. She was almost as tall as I was. My heart was pounding. I put my hands on her waist. Our lips met. We kissed softly at first, then harder. The elevator reached the lobby. The doors opened for a minute and then closed. We were still kissing.

'I have to see you again,' I said as I walked with my arm around her to the street. She gave me her phone number. She reached up and kissed me again. I held her close and her hair fell against my face. I could inhale her scent and feel the softness of her cheek against mine.

'I have to tell you something, something that Andrew does not know. I'm *katoey*,' she said softly in my ear.

'What's that?'

'I'll explain over dinner tomorrow, if you call me.'

She climbed into the cab, her skirt riding even higher up her hips, showing off her long shapely legs. *Katoey*? I didn't care what province she came from or what religion she was, all I knew was that I could not wait until tomorrow.

I Love Thailand

I enjoy reading the newspapers which I do every day online. I read the *New York Post* and *The New York Times*, whose motto is 'All the news that's fit to print.' The *New York Post* covers colorful local news, stories that would never make it to *The New York Times*.

Today I read a story about a prostitution ring that was busted in Manhattan. This is not unusual and these services can be found everywhere. What really astounded me was the fact that the madam was asking for and receiving US$1,400 for two girls at once, short time, and one of the girls arrested was thirty-seven years old.

Let me say that again US$1,400! Thirty-seven years old! Unbelievable for those of us who live in Thailand. Jeez, I haven't been to America in a long time but this price is ridiculous. My friend Fat Larry who lives there and visits Thailand every year says he does not bother to even think about dating in New York. It's way too expensive and the girls are snooty. He does go to a local bordello once or twice a year and the tariff is US$260 for half an hour, so I guess he's getting a bargain. For the same price, if you go to Kata or Karon in Phuket you can get eight girls for the entire night, including bar fine. As for the cost of female companionship, at Nana in Bangkok the girls get 1,500 to 2,000 baht short time and 600 baht bar fine.

I think we have all been saying that the prices are going up in Nana but when you look at costs worldwide—and I only look at New York prices—it's a gift from God to be able to live here.

Leave your boots and cold weather clothes at home. The weather is always nice in Thailand.

When I go to Bangkok I always stay at the Majestic Suites Hotel on Sukhumvit Road, between Soi Four and the Landmark Hotel. A very nice room there is about 1,400 baht or about US$36. You can't park your car in New York for that price, let alone get a room. I think the cheapest room one might be able to obtain in NYC would be about US$130.

I have to say I feel very lucky to live in Thailand. I was thinking about that when I went to a dental surgery in Chalong today and the technician was German, so I knew that I would receive quality work. I was putting off having a crown replaced so was delighted to find the lab, and what do you think he is charging me? Fifteen hundred baht! Okay, I ended up bypassing the dentist so I could save money, but this is so cheap it's silly. Back in America it would be US$1,500—not baht.

Again, comparing Bangkok and New York they are both sophisticated large cities with plenty of cultural events and excellent restaurants. My very favorite is the Zanotti Ristorante Italiano on Soi Saladaeng. The food, service and setting are superb with lower prices than one would expect. Auberge Dab French Restaurant on Ploenchit Road is also good. They have a fixed-price lunch for under 400 baht and a terrific set-price dinner for 1,200 baht. The JW Marriott Hotel just down the street has a buffet lunch for 800 baht that's magnificent.

The food at these places will knock your socks off, is reasonably priced and I will put these places up against any restaurant in America. You don't have to visit Bangkok to find international restaurants, given the amount of expatriates arriving to Thailand from all over the world. Even small towns in the north have German, Italian, Mexican, and Indian restaurants and eating places of every kind and price. And how about the pleasant service here in Thailand and the friendly smiles.

Thais use the word 'sanuk' to mean everthing that is fun, and they incorporate it into every facet of their lives. If only the people back home took the time to smile and have a bit of fun like the

Thais, America would be a better place.

I have a house in Phuket and sometimes need an electrician or a plumber or someone to cut the grass. Admittedly a good man is hard to find but when you do, the prices are very, very reasonable. I can always find a few Thai guys hanging around if I need some work around the yard. I pay them 100 baht an hour and everyone is happy. For eight hours that would be 800 baht, or about twenty bucks. My brother who lives in New York State needed some work done in his yard and drove to a corner where illegal immigrants wait to be picked up. They get US$100 a day now, and when my brother's worker saw a shovel in the car he demanded US$125.

I needed assistance around the house so I hired a live-in lady right off the bus from Roi Et. I should really say 'girl'. She makes me breakfast and dinner, feeds my three dogs and one cat, goes shopping for their food, cooks the chicken and fish that I buy for them, cleans the house every day and does the laundry. I was in the shower today when she was scrubbing me down and I was thinking how luxurious I feel having this kind of help. I understand that the rates here for something like this are 8,000 baht a month. I have a friend that pays 6,000 baht a month. I am paying this girl 10,000 baht a month and my neighbors are crying that I am over paying her. This is plain foolish. I want her to be happy and happy she is. I am going to take her out for dinner tonight along with three of her friends. They want to eat at a local Isaan restaurant. I am going to be hailed a 'big sport' for simply paying a price so reasonable it's embarrassing.

I took my car to be repaired in the S&P Body Shop in Rawai. I had dents in three fenders, two doors, the trunk, and both bumpers. A lot of work. They did a super job and only charged me 12,000 baht. Hell, I paid more than that for my cell phone. The downside of this is that Thais tend to run into your car even if you are parked or waiting for a red light. Car tires are much cheaper here and gasoline is half the cost that it is in America.

I am not a fan of Indian tailors and the ones in my neighborhood are second-rate, but when I was in Bangkok I had four cotton dress shirts made for 1,250 baht each—that's about US$32—and I am delighted with them. I haven't bought a good dress shirt since I was in New York in 1986 and paid US$55 for a shirt off the rack. I can't imagine how much it would cost to have a shirt made there now.

Medical care, hospitals and doctors in Thailand are a third of the cost of the United States—or less. I had my inner ear checked at a doctor's office in New York City. It took about ten minutes and it cost US$250. I had the same problem in Phuket and went to a hospital and the doctor charged me 400 baht or about ten bucks. Now, that's quite a difference.

I haven't even mentioned the beaches which are the best in the world and the spectacular limestone cliffs surrounding the Hat Rai Leh beaches. Go to the Caribbean Islands? I don't think so when the beaches here are just as nice and you can stay for a month for the cost of a few days in a fancy hotel in Saint Barts.

Land of Opportunity

I was coming out of the supermarket in Rawai, Phuket when a *farang* guy wished me a big hello and introduced himself. He was Bill from Canada, was building a bar and invited me to the soft opening the next week. He pointed across the street to a modest, round, brick bar almost finished with a thatched roof, one fridge and two restrooms. I asked him if he was going to have girls there. He said he hadn't decided yet. I was just curious as right opposite was a large girlie bar with pool tables, live music on the weekends, a free buffet, and plenty of girls. Just down the street, about fifty feet away, was a family-type expat bar that had very solid clientele. I wondered what niche he thought he was going to fit into. As it turned out, it really didn't matter.

'How long have you been here?' he asked.

I said about eight years.

'You have a Thai wife?'

'No.'

'But you have a Thai girlfriend?'

'No.'

Bill shook his head and looked at me as if I was a feeble-minded schmuck. Been here eight years and no girl. Then his face brightened. 'I've only been here two weeks and I have a beautiful girlfriend. Not only that but I'm making her dreams come true.' He needed no prodding from me as he continued, proud and happy as could be. 'All her life she wanted her own bar and now I'm building one for her.'

Well, I thought, isn't that what all the bargirls want? I edged towards my car but Bill wasn't letting me get away just yet.

'I'm too smart to get involved in all that work permit stuff so

I put the bar in her name and I'll direct it from behind the scenes. I can't afford to retire yet so this income will be a big help in letting me stay here.' As soon as he said he would direct from behind the scenes I knew he was doomed. A bargirl with her own bar is going to listen to him? I was trying not to look at him as if he were the feeble-minded one.

I dropped into his bar the following week but Bill was not there. 'Bill go eat,' said the attractive girl behind the bar. I stopped a few more times but never found Bill. Then I saw a 'For Sale' sign hung over the bar. I stopped and asked where Bill was.

'I finish him' was the girl's reply. Well, so much for Bill but an opportunity for me, I thought.

Now I must digress a bit and go back in time to another story. About seven years ago I met one of the most beautiful girls on the island. Yes, I know everyone says that. Soopies and I had a wonderful three months together. One day she told me she loved me very much and that we should date for one year, then get married and after another year we would have children. We could buy a house now and move in together. (I pay for it and it goes in her name, of course.) I declined her offer and the next day she dropped me as flat as yesterday's pancake. Today she owns four houses. It looks to me like buying a house for her is similar to Spider Woman's kiss of death.

However, we are still friends and when she is between boyfriends she gives me a call and we go out. Not long ago I took her to Pattaya for five days. While we were there she asked me if I wanted to move in with her, but there were just two small items to take care of. Her monthly expenses were 35,000 baht and I would have to leave my two dogs behind. Leave my two faithful friends? They always stay home and wait for me, never go out and never ask for anything, and I am quite sure of their love for me. No way would I do that. If I had deeper pockets I would just give her the 35,000 every month, I really would.

We were talking about her future and what she would do. She

confided that she was freelancing out of the VIP in Patong and was asking for and often receiving 5,000 baht per night, which is high for Phuket but if you were a tourist working back in the States and here on vacation, you wouldn't think twice about it. A girl like her back in New York City would cost you 5,000 all right, but it would be dollars, believe me. What she was doing was not what you would call 'steady work' and she was thinking of opening a bar to earn a living.

Back to the present.

I called and told her we would look at this bar for sale. I had no intention of buying her a bar. My friends would laugh me out of town. I would be too embarrassed to leave my house. I would have to go hide out with Bill in Canada. But I did figure that this would be good for a few days of love stuff as we negotiated the deal. I thought that if Thai girls can pull our strings, to turn it around is fair play.

On the way to the bar Soopies explained that she would bring down a dozen girls from Udon Thani. It would cost 2,000 a girl, a thousand for the madam and 1,000 for the bus fare. We would need to rent a small house for the girls to stay in and we would have to feed them and pay them a salary. (Read: Frank would pay for everything.)

We arrived at the bar and I was surprised to see that the attractive bargirl owner spoke perfect English.

'Okay, how much do you want for the bar?'

'Three hundred thousand baht.'

'What? Are you crazy?' I said. Actually I was a bit relieved that the price was so outrageous. There was no way we would pay that amount and I would be off the hook, so to speak, but still look like a good guy.

'My boyfriend pay 4,000,' said the bar owner.

And I believed her. The place could not have cost more than 60,000 or 80,000 so she'd probably got about 200,000 from the contractor who'd made a handsome profit himself.

'Listen,' I said. 'If you want a bar so much why don't you just stay here and run it yourself?'

'What?' she said indignantly. 'I can't stay here. I have a husband and son in America. I just come for one month to visit my mother.' I just stood there in awe. Within a month she'd got a guy, opened a bar and was now trying to sell it. She'd maybe pocket close to half a million baht in her bank account. You really have to give them credit. Give these girls an education, turn them loose in America and they would be running the country.

As for what happened to Soopies, I was never really worried. She met a dentist from Germany at the VIP. A very nice-looking man about thirty-five years old, first time in Thailand. She stayed with him for five days and never asked for a dime. Took him to her house, introduced him to her mother and her six-year-old daughter. Soopies was a good girl whose previous boyfriend had left her suddenly with bills to pay.

'I love you and want to be completely honest with you,' she told the dentist. 'I want to wait for you but I may have to work in a bar and go with a man. I don't want to. I have never done this but I need to survive. When you come back in three months you may find me in a bar and I don't want you to be angry with me.'

'How much do you need?'

'Thirty-five thousand.'

The guy took the cash right out of his pocket and handed it to her, promising to send her more. When he got home his friend, who had been to Thailand before, gave him holy hell and called him a moron.

I happened to be driving Soopies to a wine-tasting session when the dentist called from Germany. He felt that she'd lied to him and he would not be sending any money. Soopies had a fit. She said she was going to send him his 35,000 the next day. He could keep his money and she would never see him again. Then she sobbed into the telephone. When she closed her cell phone she looked at me and smiled, shrugging her shoulders. Time would tell.

The end of the story is that he not only sent the money but also brought her to Germany for three months. She hated it there. Cold and boring. But after all, the guy was still sending the 35,000 a month. She came to my house later to ask for advice. He wanted to get married but she was tired of him already. The deal was she had to spend three months a year in Germany and he would come to Thailand for three months.

'Soopies,' I said. 'You're not getting any younger and you will still have six months a year all to yourself.'

They got married and he bought her a large home in one of the Land and House developments. A happy ending for everyone, except Bill from Canada.

Rain in Rawai

It's been raining so much all week you could almost roll up the streets at night. Songkhran is long over and Visakha Puja Day has passed. My last name, Visakay, had an 'h' in it but my grandfather took it out to Americanize it when he moved over from Middle Europe. If it was still there all you would have to do would be to add a 'y' at the end and I would be part of the holiday. My wise friend Dana keeps telling me that I am part Indian.

If I want to go out for a drink or pick up a girl I have to go to Kata or Karon. There is nothing happening in sleepy Rawai. So one night I drove over the hill to check out the scene. There wasn't much happening there either; half of the bars were closed and most of the bargirls had gone home—at least all the good-looking ones that had made some money during high season. Nothing left but girls—or should I say women—that were average and below average. If there *was* a better-than-average girl there she acted like she was a beauty queen. However, after searching I found a real cutie and asked her the four standard questions:

We take shower together?

You can smoke?

You can stay all night?

Are you afraid of dogs?

These are all important questions, especially the last one as I had one girl that started to quiver and shake when she got to my house and ran into my German Shepherd that was much bigger than she was. I had to take her back to the bar.

We made a deal at 1,000 baht for the night and I took her home. When we arrived she said she did not want to take a shower. I was trying to be more patient so I let it go. We were almost into bed when she said she had to go back in an hour and could not stay. That was it. I picked up her clothes and threw them at her.

'Get dressed. Get out.'

'What? What's the matter?' They lie to you, make up their own rules and then don't understand when you become angry.

I took her back. I stopped the car a block from the bar so she had to walk a bit and threw her out. I lost the 200-baht bar fine but she did not get 1,000 from me, so we're more than even.

Now I hate going to Patong. It's just too far to drive. I don't like to do short time there as I would rather be comfortable at home in my own bed, so I pay a little more and take the girl home for the whole night to avoid going back and forth twice in one night. The one thing that I have to say is that you can always find a beauty or two in Patong.

I also have to say that the girls—as pretty as they are—have been in the business a while and are all wise guys or close to it. No shy newcomers there. So I bit the bullet and off I went. The bars under the Tiger Disco have all the attractive girls. But this changes—for years it was Soi Eric. There was this girl, Sai, with her slacks slung low on her hips and from the back you could clearly see the top of her thong underpants. She also had her blouse tied up revealing a flat stomach. I don't know about you but this combination is irresistible to me.

I made a deal with her: 2,000 baht for the whole night, and off we went, but she said she had to go back and give her girlfriend the motorcycle key. It took a while to get to Rawai and we made boom-boom after taking a shower. We were about to step into the shower again when her phone rang. She answered it and then handed it to me. 'It's for you.'

Her girlfriend shouted, 'Sai must come right back. Have big problem at bar.' I gave Sai her phone so she could get the news first-hand. They sure have the timing down, I thought. Of course, she had told her friend to call. She did not need to give her a motorcycle key. Sai apologized as she was getting dressed.

'No problem,' I said, even though Patong was a long way off and I had just come from there. When we were about to leave I handed her 1,000 baht.

'What's this?' she exclaimed.

'My darling, I'm sorry you can do only short time so I can't pay you for all night.'

'Not my fault. Pay me 2,000.' Funny how they can understand doing only half a job but can't understand not getting paid for the whole job.

'Sorry, not my fault either. You want to stay, I will pay you 2,000.'

'No, I have to go back.' I walked her to the front gate and closed and locked the gate behind her.

'What are you doing? You're going to drive me back, aren't you?'

'No, my darling. I'm too tired now. If you want to sleep here I will drive you back tomorrow.'

'But I have to go back.'

'Yes, you do—but I don't. I said that I would take you back tomorrow and I will, but not tonight.'

'How will I get back to Patong?'

I pointed to some bar lights off in the distance. 'Motorcycle taxi there, take you back.' I didn't know if there was a motorbike there or not but I wanted to get rid of her.

'Give me money for cab.'

Just to make her nuts I said, 'You have 1,000 already—you have enough money.'

But then I relented and gave her 200 baht and she stormed off while I headed to bed. I'm sure they charged her more than 200 for a trip to Patong.

No, I was not harsh with the girl. Next time, don't lie if you don't want to do short time. Just tell me. She wanted to have her cake and eat it, so to speak. Let her learn a lesson and only screw with the two-weekers.

More Rain in Rawai

It's been raining every day for four weeks. At night it really pours down. Rawai is all but closed in the evenings and a quick trip to Kata or Karon reveals the same lack of activity. If there are any tourists here, they sure aren't arriving on their rented Honda Dreams in this weather. After my last experience driving to Patong I wasn't too anxious to give it another go, but I was getting cabin fever sitting around day after day so off I went for another try. I arrived at Soi Bangla around ten at night. A bit early but I really don't like to stay out too late. There wasn't much going on there either; a bunch of average women in the bars and not many at that. Most of the pretty girls had left weeks ago. The bars under the Tiger Disco still seemed to have the most attractive girls and I found a beauty—twenty years old with those tight short shorts and a killer smile, not much English, but you could see that she was hip to the scene, even if she was a new arrival. We agreed on 2,000 baht for the night and back to Rawai we went. All went well and she was really nice. Maybe my luck was changing for the better.

I was driving her back to Patong the next day and had an idea. Since I was so bored and didn't want to drive back and forth, I asked if she wanted to stay for a few days. We settled on 2,000 a night for the first two nights and 1,500 for each of the following two nights. I was to pick her up that same evening. When I called on the way over she said to meet her in front of Ocean Shopping Plaza on Soi Bangla.

'Let's go inside. I want to show you something,' she said when I arrived. Off we went to the women's department where she tried on a fancy 1,500-baht pair of shoes covered with rhinestones.

'Do you like them?'

'*Chok dee*,' I said. (I thought, if she thinks I'm springing for those shoes, she's crazy.) She came back to reality and settled for a 200-baht pair. Of course, it's a given if you go shopping with a Thai girl, you pay.

We were driving back to my house and I mentioned that I was flying to Bangkok at the end of the week and would stay for four days.

'Can I go with you?'

'Sure you can but since the airfare is 8,400 baht round trip, (I fly business class) it's a wash. I will take you—but not pay you for those nights.'

'All right, but I need one day off to see my friends.'

'Fine. I will go see my friends also.' (Nana Plaza, here I come.)

'Can my girlfriend come to Bangkok with us?'

At 8,000 baht a ticket I had no intention of taking another person but I said, 'Is your girlfriend going to make me boom-boom every night?'

'No, just friend.'

'Santa Claus comes at Christmas. She will have to wait.' I don't know if Thais understand the concept of this as they can hardly speak English, but I like to say it and they get the idea anyway. We hadn't even spent the first of our four nights together and she was already shooting at me with both barrels, which I found annoying.

We stopped at Don's Restaurant in Rawai for a bite to eat, ran into a few people I know then went to my house and spent a very pleasant evening together. We woke up the next morning and started to dress as I was going to take her to the Thai Airways office in Phuket and buy her a round-trip ticket.

Suddenly she says to me, 'If you are not going to pay me in Bangkok, can you take me shopping when we go there?'

'No, thank you.' Another one of my favorite sayings. I was

thinking that this girl was becoming more and more annoying as time went on. As was I was paying her 7,000 baht for four days, then another 8,000 for her airfare. If only these girls could relax a bit and not go all out for the kill they might get further, I thought. But who knows? I doubt you could explain that to them anyway.

'Can we go to Patong first. I want my girlfriend to come with us to Phuket.'

'Why?' I didn't take this girl for four days so I could drive back and forth to Patong every day. I wanted to avoid that.

'We can do some shopping together in Phuket.' (Wait! I thought. She thinks that she is going to get me to take both of them shopping?)

'And how will she get back to Patong?'

'You can drive her.'

'No, thank you.'

'Okay, she take bus back.'

I drive my girl to Patong and on the way give her 2,000 baht. 'I will pay you every day,' I said. I dropped her off so she could run in and pick up her girlfriend, then I drove away. I was thinking that I would quit while I was ahead, or at least not too far behind. She called me on my cell phone. I told her the deal was off. She sounded sad, upset and confused all at the same time. I guess she thought that she had captured a willing victim.

My Thai is not good enough to tell her that she is a scheming little so-and-so.

The next day I was having lunch at Don's when I ran into two of my friends—well, more like acquaintances. One of them, Randy Worthless, has been coming here twice a year for a few years and this time he had brought a friend with him, Roger, a first-timer. Now Randy is not the brightest boy on the block and after all those trips to Thailand, he's still a bit naive. He'd picked up his present girl in Long Gun, Soi Cowboy. He bar fined her right out, even though she said she was only a waitress and never went with men. It was only because she found him so attractive.

He went back a few times and mostly she was out, 'picking up soda for the bar.' That's what they told him. Anyway, he told me he wanted to bring her to Phuket. She told him that he had to buy her out of the bar to the tune of 20,000 baht, and since she is a good girl he had to send her mother another 20,000. Randy fell for the whole bunch of nonsense so I figured that he wasn't exactly the right person to show the new guy around. But, okay, none of my business.

The two of them sat down at my table and made small talk for a few minutes before getting right to the point.

'That girl you were with yesterday is a real knockout.'

I nodded my head.

'Where is she? Is she still with you?' Roger was drooling at the mouth.

'I took her back.'

'Would you mind if I went out with her?'

I shrugged my shoulders. I didn't care.

'Under the Tiger in Patong. Third bar on the left. Her name is Nuit.'

I saw Randy a week later. Roger had gone back to Hawaii. Randy usually stays for a few months.

'Roger had a great time with that girl, really fell in love. Kept her all week.' I nodded my head. I didn't care.

Randy continued: 'Roger is such a great guy. You know what he did?' I shrugged my shoulders. I didn't care.

'He found out that Nuit has breast cancer and it will kill her if she doesn't have an operation. She can't afford it so she was going back to Khorat to die with her family. My friend only knows her for a week but what does he do? He gives her US$2,000 for the operation just before he leaves. Saves her life. Is he a great guy or what?'

I nodded my head.

Randy's Refrain

Randy had just got divorced for the third time and had come to Thailand to gain back some of his self-esteem. He felt that he was a failure with women and had heard that Thai girls were sweet and loving. Back in America he worked hard and went out occasionally but at fifty-seven years old, he just couldn't connect with younger girls. They looked right past him or acted puzzled when he spoke to them. He was a nice-looking man, something like an older John Denver, but when he visited a disco or club many of the girls he spoke to assumed that he was looking for his daughter. His wife had informed him of their divorce by fax from another state and his two daughters had soon moved out of the house, one into the arms of a drug dealer. Randy was feeling pretty unloved and needed some companionship.

He preferred to swim and go to the beach but since he had a stopover in Bangkok on the way to Phuket, he decided to check out the nightlife. He couldn't wait and went to the Long Gun Bar on Soi Cowboy, off Sukhumvit Road. The bar was dark and Dumi was the very first girl Randy saw as he walked in. She was standing against the wall near the door. She smiled at him. Randy thought that she looked so sweet and innocent.

'You are such a beautiful girl, what are you doing here?'

'I come here see friend. I not bargirl. Sometimes I bring drink to customer.'

'Can you come to my hotel?'

'I never go with *farang* before.'

Randy fell in love immediately and wanted to take Dumi with him to Phuket. She was not sure if she could go and had to obtain permission from the bar owner. Forty thousand was the buy-out price explained to him by the owner because he had met her at the bar. Randy paid the bar fine and he and Dumi spent a wonderful month in Phuket. When Randy had to fly back to America he gave Dumi 20,000 baht and put her on a plane to Udon Thani to stay with her parents until he was able to return. He went back to Bangkok a few months later and stopped in at the Long Gun. He was surprised to see Dumi standing against the wall in exactly the same spot as before. She had been working at the bar in order to earn money to send to her parents, she explained. She had also borrowed 40,000 baht from the mamma-san to send home and she could not leave unless she paid it back. Randy gave her the money and took Dumi to Phuket.

Randy loved the island and bought a house. Foreigners were not allowed to own land, so to make the process simpler he put the house in Dumi's name. He would go back to America, sell his business and stay in paradise with Dumi forever. She asked if she could have her parents visit while he was away. A good idea, he thought. Dumi would be safe and happy. He called Dumi every week from America. She assured him that everything was fine but she needed 40,000 baht to cover expenses. Randy sent the money right away.

When he went back to his house in Phuket the first thing that he saw were two children playing in the front yard. Dumi's parents were inside sitting on the floor eating, along with her aunt, uncle and a nice-looking young man. Dumi introduced everyone and Randy sat down on the floor next to her parents. He was delighted to be back, even if the house was fuller then he had anticipated.

'Who are the kids outside?' he asked.

'They're mine,' replied Dumi.

'You never told me that you had children.'

'You never asked me. Aren't my children welcome?'

'Of course they are, my darling. How long are your parents and aunt and uncle planning on staying?'

'They live here now.'

'All of them?'

'Yes, they are my family.'

'And the young man, who is he?'

'Oh, that's my husband. He will stay here also.'

'Your husband? You never told me that you were married.'

'I would have told you if you had asked me.'

'Dumi, you said that you loved me and that you wanted to stay with me forever.'

'I do.'

'What about everyone else? Where is everyone sleeping?'

'Well, we have two bedrooms and a living room, so we are all comfortable. Besides, this house very large compared ours in Udon.'

Randy was confused and disturbed. He picked up his suitcase. 'Where are we sleeping? In which room?' Dumi led Randy to the storage room. It had a cement floor and contained the hot-water heater and some gardening tools. Dumi pointed to a small folding cot. 'You can stay here.'

'What? Are you crazy?' Randy exclaimed. 'I want everyone out of here right now.'

'You want problem? I can give you one,' Dumi said as she punched some numbers into her cell phone. Randy sat down on the cot. He felt dizzy and disorientated. It was Kafkaesque, he thought. He felt as if he might turn into a large beetle, crawl under the cot and stay there. He held his head in his hands, trying to figure out what was happening.

'You,' a loud voice said. Randy looked up. A police officer in a tight-fitting brown uniform stood over him. Thank God, now he would get things straightened out. The officer took him outside. Randy started to explain to the policeman: 'The house is mine. I bought it. I want everyone to get out—her too.' Randy pointed to Dumi. Dumi put Randy's suitcase on the street. She had brought some papers from the house and was pointing to the top of one of the pages. Randy could see it was all in Thai.

The officer took him by the arm. 'Lady have papers for house—her house. You want to go to jail? You stay here, I take you.'

It was all too much for Randy. He picked up his suitcase and walked off. He wandered down the road in a daze, not knowing where he was going. He came to an open-air bar. A few girls lounged on rattan chairs.

A drink would surely do him good, he thought. Randy ordered a scotch and soda. Then he saw her, sitting across the bar. She smiled at him. She was so sweet and innocent-looking.

'You are such a beautiful girl. What are you doing here?' he said.

Hmm, Roast Dog

I don't think that I would like to see a dog slaughtered, nor any other animal. It would do nothing for my appetite. However if one did want to eat dog, Vietnam or China would be the place to go. Once I went to an open-air market in Guangzhou, China. It's about ten square blocks and if something's edible (or not) you can find it there. Refrigeration not being the uppermost in people's minds, many animals are sold alive. They are kept in tiny cages made of twigs or branches. Sometimes buyers bring their own cages. Can't get fresher food than that, can you.

There were so many animals that at first I thought I had come across a pet center. But then I noticed all the weasels, rodents, bats—the type of things one normally wouldn't keep as pets. There were hundreds of snakes, big and small. Bugs half the size of your fist with legs so long they were tied with long pieces of grass. They were also selling about a million smaller bugs, some alive, some already cooked. What I remember most was a large, whole smoked dog hanging upside down.

It was my first trip to Asia and I was not quite ready to eat these things. Later I traveled to Hanoi. There were a number of restaurants just outside of town near Bay Mau Lake. Like many of the homes in rural Vietnam, these old wooden restaurant buildings were on stilts and had a bunch of dogs underneath. How cute, I thought. The owner keeps his pets at work with him. I liked the idea and stopped there one day to eat. The restaurant only sold sausages and dried meat. I had some of both. The dried meat was tough and the sausages were past their prime, so I didn't eat much. It was only later that I learned I was eating some of those cute dogs I'd seen earlier; that was what these restaurants specialized in.

I stayed in the old section of Hanoi and there was a small outdoor market down an alleyway right next door to my accommodation. There was a smoked dog hanging there. It was golden brown, like a roasted pig. It looked so good that I thought I would give it another try. It was delicious—moist and tender. The skin tasted a bit like pork and the meat somewhat like beef.

I found out later that it's relatively expensive in Hanoi. I paid a dollar for a bunch of cut up pieces wrapped in newspaper along with a tiny plastic bag of hot sauce. I brought the package back to my modest hotel and when the two boys that worked there saw what I had they went crazy, laughing and whooping, rolling on the floor. When they got over their merriment (they had never heard of a foreigner eating dog before) they asked if they could eat some too. That's when they told me it cost so much it was out of their reach.

I will not say too much about eating bugs as we all know about that. It was a while before a bargirl explained to me that there was a proper way to eat each one. First you pull all those scratchy legs off the grasshoppers and big fat water bugs. You only eat the inside which is about as big as the end of your thumb, soft and yellow and tastes a bit like sweet almonds. The rest of the insects I came across seemed to be sprayed with soy sauce and had a flavor like crunchy Japanese bar snacks. Not all that interesting.

Once, I took a local boat trip up the Chao Phraya River, Thailand to the last stop. I got off, walked about the town a bit and came to an open-air market. At a food stand people were roasting rats on a stick, the rats spread out like they were on a cross. I bought one to take away and was given some *phrik nam pla* to go with it. I sat on a bench wishing that I had at least a knife to cut a piece of it off. The top of the leg looked the best and I bit into it. The skin was tough and the meat almost as tough. I chewed on it then spat it out. A failed experiment. I just think that it was overcooked and may give this delicacy another try some day.

In Siem Reap, Cambodia I sat by a river in a little market and enjoyed foamy home-made beer out of a bamboo cup while watching a barbecue. I ate fish, frogs and eel. There were also snakes roasting with their stomachs slit open, five or six small yellow eggs along the inside of each snake. Okay, I thought, I'll try one of those. The eggs were tender, just like boiled chicken egg yolks but the meat was tough and stuck to the tiny ribs—impossible to eat.

The very best snake that I ever ate was rattlesnake in Jackson Hole, Wyoming. Tender white meat sauteed in butter with tomato, lemon and capers, Provençal style. I thought that if I simmered a snake long enough the meat would fall off the bone and I could do the same thing here in Thailand. My neighbor was building some houses and was always complaining about the cobras moving about in the undergrowth. I told him I needed a big one. He brought a whopper over two days later. It was, at the very least, three feet long and fat. I nailed the head to a tree, sliced the skin around the neck and peeled the skin right off. A piece of cake so far. I cut the head off. There wasn't much of a stomach to clean out and I coiled the snake into a pot and covered it with chicken stock. I don't think it was cheating to use canned chicken stock as I use it for everything.

I simmered that damn snake for three hours and the meat was still not tender. Losing my patience I took it out, chopped it into three-inch pieces and simmered it some more. I added chopped tomato, pieces of mango, parsley, garlic, lime juice and a bunch of spices. After another hour the meat was still on the bone.

As I had promised my friends dinner I thought, what the hell I'll serve it as soup. It was very colorful and didn't look too bad, I must say. My friends had to suck on the snake ribs but everyone that was brave enough to try it liked it and a Thai girl told me it was especially good. I took that as a big compliment and never mentioned the Campbell's chicken soup.

In Phnom Penh, I came across a sidewalk food stand where a lady was deep frying baby birds. The birds had been plucked and washed and you ate them whole. You could have them plain or dipped in batter. I had always wanted to try these. I ordered one of each. They were not too meaty and a bit bony as you ate the beak, head and legs—everything.

I thought I was safe from food poisoning as the meat was cooked to order but I did not think about how long they had been sitting there and the next day I was as sick as a dog. Just as well, I suppose, as I went to the big yellow Central Market where they were selling cooked black spiders as large as the back of your hand. These spiders were so fat that all you had to do was pull off a few of the legs and bite right in. But I was in no condition to eat and who knew how long they'd been sitting in the sun.

The only really strange thing that I'd tasted back home in New York was when I went over to a Japanese friend's house for some holiday or other. About eight of us were seated at the dining-room table when someone brought out a large turtle, cut its throat and let it bleed into a pot. Jeez, this is one hell of a start to dinner, I thought. I wonder what's coming next. He poured the blood into shot glasses and then gave each one of us a shot of clear Japanese rice whisky. We drank one shot after the other. The blood tasted like, well, blood and the whiskey tasted like it could peel the paint right off your car. The turtle then came back as pieces in soup. It was tender and the meat was green. I even received a tiny piece of liver.

Actually the most fun I've ever had eating something strange was in New York where one can find authentic and delicious foreign food. I took a Jewish girlfriend downtown to Little Italy for dinner and I ordered half a goat's head. She heard me order it but never imagined that was what it actually was. It's pretty tasty as you get some of the brains and the cheek meat is delicious. I have to admit it was a bit nasty-looking when it came to the table. The lips were curled back exposing the teeth in a gruesome grimace and the tongue was hanging out. I plunged my fork in, plucked out an eyeball and popped it into my mouth. My girlfriend sprang from the table and didn't come out of the ladies' room for twenty minutes.

Offal? I've eaten all of it: hearts, lungs, intestines, tripe, thymus, liver (foie gras, sauteed, please God more) calves' brains with black butter in France and bulls' testicles in Spain. Sea slugs, fat white bamboo grubs, snails and worms. Corn fungus and tiny white ants' eggs in Mexico, both of which are delicacies (of course). I want to eat whale. My apologies to anyone who's politically correct out there. Human flesh? Have you ever taken a good look at the inside of your girlfriend's thigh? That's all I'm going to say about that.

A few things I will draw the line at though. Bush meat— gorillas, monkeys and such—ethically wrong.

Jerry Hopkins, a wonderful character and superb storyteller, once served his wife's baby's placenta in the form of a pâté to his friends. Mmm. Okay, maybe with a good cracker or a few capers. For those interested in this kind of thing Jerry has a great book out called *Strange Foods*, published by Periplus Editions. I can also recommend a superior cookbook, *Unmentionable Cuisine* by Calvin W. Schwabe, published by University of Virginia Press.

Happy eating.

Truth in Advertising

No, I'm not suggesting a yellow star be pinned to the jackets of vendors. It's not like that at all, but we do need some help. After all, what's fair is fair. It should be fair for the buyer and fair for the seller. I understand that many of us want to be somewhere else or someone else or have a different life. I'm okay with that but let's not have my rights violated in an effort to protect theirs.

I've been living in Phuket for the past eight years and have experienced this difficulty before. It's not only the plethora of fake watches, Oakley sunglasses, Zippo lighters, Polo shirts—the list is endless. The Ralph Lauren Company confiscated thousands of fake shirts they found sold in Southeast Asia and you constantly see pictures in the papers of steamrollers flattening piles of counterfeit CDs and DVDs. And it's obvious you can't purchase a genuine Rolex on the sidewalk for 2,000 baht. Just ask the vendors if you want information—'it's all real' they'll tell you.

However, if one is selling something, there is an obligation to deliver what is presented to the buyer. As anyone can tell you, this certainly does not always happen—especially here. The Indian tailor shops marked Armani and Boss are a joke. The Cuban cigars sold in Phuket are all made in the Dominican Republic. (Except if you find any from Cigar Joe in Bangkok. Those are real and worth the expense.) Remember all the national park land that was sold here in Phuket for hundreds of thousands of dollars about four years ago? It was all marked with real Chanote titles that were issued by the local government. Go figure. There sure were a lot of disappointed people when the big boys came down from Bangkok and chased everyone off the land.

Once again it's high season. The weather is just fabulous

and it's nice to see the restaurants and bars full again. Kata and Karon are filled with tourists, most walking hand in hand along the streets, blissfully unaware that they might be run down at any second by a *tuk tuk* or a motorcycle. One has to cross over the yellow line to avoid hitting these people. No matter. The Thai drivers here are also blissfully unaware of the yellow lines or any driving regulations.

Farther along the road leads to Patong, a vacation resort filled with couples and families, beer bars, hookers, transvestites, crowded beaches and over-priced restaurants. Only Pattaya is a worse choice to take your children or new bride. How do they get here I wonder? Who sends them? These stocky *farang*s and Korean couples who seem to be happy walking down a broken sidewalk, pushing past Indian tailors calling to them, dodging the touts with leaflets of girly shows and massage parlors?

I drove to Karon the other night and it was so busy that I could not find a parking space. I ended up in a bar I had not been to before near Kata. There were a few *katoey*s at the bar and also a few cute girls. As soon as I took a seat a girl came over and asked if I would buy her a drink. A greedy girl and not a good sign. So I said to her, 'Wait a minute. Are you coming home with me tonight?'

'Yes.'

'Tonight, you come with me. Stay long time?'

'Yes.'

Having made that clear, I settled in and we had a few drinks together and later I called for the check and bar fine. The girl looked me right in the eye and smiled. I could tell I was about to be screwed.

'I sorry, have stomach ache. Can not go,' followed by a big grin. I told her that she was a crook, a thief, a bad girl, and a liar. I got up and gave the money for the drinks to the lady bar owner and told her what had happened in an annoyed and loud voice.

'See this face?' I pointed to my nose. 'You never see again.

I never come here again.' She smiled delightedly at me along with the bargirl, both as happy as could be. They'd f**ked the stupid white guy and now he was providing them with some entertainment. But really it's my fault for living in a tourist area. The locals see a white face and think: 'They are only going to be here for two weeks and they may never come back anyway, so let's screw them while we can.' Who cares about repeat business when your average customer is leaving the country in a matter of days?

I had parked the car on the road in Kata that runs alongside Club Med and there were half a dozen bars in a row. I stopped in another open-air place. A couple of pretty girls were seated on stools and there was a real beauty behind the bar. I bought her a drink and motioned for her to come around and sit next to me. I wanted a closer look at her. She was tall and slim with long, silky black hair. She had beautiful full, sensuous lips and white teeth; I was already imagining kissing her. Her name was Noi and her English was poor. No matter. She was outstanding. I noticed that there was a ladyboy at the end of the bar: dressed to kill, lots of make-up and a glittery dress.

I looked back at my girl. She was wearing slacks, a shirt and a sweater—low-key style, just what a girl new to the game would wear, not exposing herself too much. I did speak to her a bit and held her hand. She had long slim fingers and a delicate soft voice. She was twenty years old and had just come down from Chiang Mai. I asked if she had any children and she said no.

I had a bit more of my drink as the ladyboy from the end of the bar wandered by. What the hell, I thought, might as well make sure. I turned to my girl and asked her if she was *katoey*.

'What?' she replied. 'Who me?' Her eyes were wide in surprise. Jeez, this is embarrassing, I thought, but continued to push on.

'Yes, you.' I pointed to her with my finger. She looked baffled and did not reply. Well, I wanted a definite answer and asked again.

'Who me?' she said.

I replied in a louder voice. 'You! *Katoey?*' I felt like a school bully, haranguing this poor girl who probably didn't even know what I was talking about. Okay, I would stop.

The mama-san walked over to see what the problem was, why I was raising my voice.

'What?' she said. I felt awkward at making a fuss for no reason but I pressed on.

'She *katoey?*' I said, pointing to the beautiful little girl next to me who was now shyly hanging her head, looking up with big eyes.

'Yes,' the mama-san said in a matter-of-fact tone that sounded a lot like, 'Of course she is, Mr Stupid.' She then asked if I would pay the bar fine. Not this time I replied.

I just wonder what we would have done if I'd got her all the way home. I think that she was too young to have had an operation and, on reflection, she was probably wearing falsies. Do they think that you might go ahead and have sex anyway? Or will they say they have their period and opt for oral sex? Or will they say, 'I thought you knew'?

I have no idea but it's annoying as hell that I almost took her with me. Now, I'm not saying that they should wear identification tags when they walk down the street, but for God's sake, if they are selling the merchandise in a bar or anywhere else it should be labeled. We don't have this problem back home in New York. The guys in drag look exactly like, well, guys in drag.

Maybe we can get all these 'girls' together in one or two bars and keep them there. Maybe instead of a yellow star they can wear a yellow butterfly. Wait, they should wear the butterfly at all times. Good for them and good for us, as they say here. They can identify each other and we can identify them.

The national slogan here should be changed from 'Thailand, Land Of Smiles' to 'Thailand, Caveat Emptor.'

The Pleasures of
High Season in Phuket

If you live here you will not look forward to high season. The streets are clogged with traffic. Your favorite, quiet little restaurant is jam-packed. Children run amok while their parents forget their manners and ignore their offspring. The beaches are packed. The cost of renting a beach chair goes from 100 to 200 baht—if you can find an empty one. Prices are automatically raised by ten per cent or much more then people 'forget' to bring them back down in March.

Is that what's troubling you buddy? Listen to me. It's not the circumstances, it's how you perceive them that counts. I eat out early to escape the crowds and also go shopping at Central or Lotus early in the morning. One day I went shopping with an older English fellow and he was outraged to see two young guys walking around the department store without shirts, like they were still at the beach. My friend questioned their manners and demanded they wear the proper attire. They told him to get stuffed and he was hopping mad. A comedy, I thought, only to be viewed in high season.

'You can't make a silk purse out of a sow's ear,' I reminded my friend. Even more interesting was when I went to the local outdoor market and saw a buxom blonde shopping in a skimpy bikini. The Thai guys couldn't stop staring while the female stall owners looked aghast. I'm going to have to buy a video camera soon. Only in high season can things like this happen.

I often eat in my friend Don's restaurant here in Rawai. This is not some bamboo shack on the beach but a nice restaurant. Often during the day or even at night visitors come in wearing just bathing suits, no shoes, sandals, or shirts.

I think it's inappropriate to dress this way, especially in the evening. But I try to have some fun with it. I stop by their tables with a big smile and inquire, 'How's the water?' Sometimes they even look down at their glasses on the table. 'Didn't you just go swimming?' I innocently inquire in a soft voice. The usual answer is 'No.' Then I apologize and go on my way. I find you can say almost anything to people if you speak politely and calmly and the important thing is to keep walking. No confrontations that way. Sometimes I even allow myself to say, 'Gotcha' when I'm far enough enough away. Am I educating these people about the error of their ways? I doubt it. Stupid is as stupid does, as Forest Gump says.

All of the expats that I know here in Phuket can't wait for the tourists to go home. Personally I take this time to go hunting. For what? you ask. I love to read and Asia Books does not have a branch here in Phuket. We only have Bookazine and The Books which carry the usual assortment of John Grisham, Robert Ludlum and Clive Cussler paperbacks. Ho-hum.

But there is a high influx of travelers in high season, and some of them bring books that are worth reading: books that have been nominated for the UK's Booker Prize, the Guardian First Book Award, or been favorably reviewed in *The New York Times*. These are enjoyed by readers on vacation and after they finish them, they leave these treasures in their rooms where they are immediately scooped up by the housekeeping staff and brought to the nearest used-book store to be sold for a profit of a few baht. It's usually twenty baht a book, which is later marked up to 200 or 300 baht. I'm not complaining, no indeed. This is the time of year that I visit most of the used-book stores in Phuket, except for the one in Kata where the woman is usually plastered out of her gourd. Have you ever been shell hunting on the beach and happen upon an unblemished beauty? What surprise, what excitement! I feel the same way when I happen upon, say, *Reading Lolita In Tehran*, *Cold Mountain* or *Slow Waltz In Cedar Bends* by Robert James Waller, who also wrote *The Bridges of Madison County.*

I used to go for walks on the beach with my girlfriend and she always liked to look for seashells, but the sad truth is that there aren't any to be found in Phuket. They were all taken long ago by the locals. Those stores by the beach with the exquisitely polished shells? They're all imported from the Philippines. I used to buy a handful of beautiful shells from those stores and drop them on the sand while walking behind my girlfriend on a lonely beach. She would never fail to be delighted on the way back when she discovered them.

The other day I was enjoying a light lunch of salad and filet of sea bass with my housekeeper at The Boathouse Hotel. It's in a beautiful location and one of the few hotels right on Kata beach. We were watching the sunbathers and swimmers—all visitors, of course. Not many Thais actually go into the ocean. All those long-legged white women with large busts in tiny bikinis walking around having the time of their lives.

'Look, look,' my companion exclaimed. 'Lady have no top, have big *nohm* (breasts).'

'Wow, thanks, my darling,' I replied. Now some may say that I was gawking while I prefer to think of it as experiencing a sociological moment. Later, Saa, my girl, pointed out a *katoey.*

'No, no my honey. I only want to see topless women.'

After lunch we strolled over to the Club Med beach, a veritable garden of bare breasts; all of those women laying on the sand, their boobs pointing skyward like ripe melons in a farmer's pasture. Actually Saa and I also enjoy watching the fat European men with tremendous beer bellies wearing bathing suits hardly big enough for a seven year old.

If you're a man that likes to check out the ladies, there's no better time than high season. Girls flood to the tourist areas from all over the country. I was in Bangkok the other day and called my favorite entertainer and where was she? Patong, Phuket, of course.

'Why?' I asked.

'Very busy here now,' she replied.

If you are going in search of a companion in Patong, there are three tiers of ladies of the evening, and all show up at different times. At eight o'clock the bars start to fill up with your normal everyday working girls, some of whom are pretty. The more attractive girls come to work after ten o'clock, not wanting to be bothered standing around waiting for a customer. The really beautiful girls do not venture out until after midnight, being freelancers who think too highly of themselves to be mere bargirls. They inhabit discos such as The Tiger, The Banana and the VIP, to name a few. You will never find an assortment of beauties like this except in high season. Think of it like a farmer coming down to reap his crops at harvest time (you are the crops and your wallet is the harvest).

During low season these beauties go back to their homes in Khon Kaen or Surin and take it easy for the rest of the year, hopefully having found at least one man to pledge their undying love to and in return receive a monthly stipend to tide them over until the following year when their suitor returns. Some girls are lucky enough to have captured the hearts (and monthly allowances) of three or four lovers then have to juggle their return visits.

It's easy to spot the tourists. Many are nicely dressed, not like the rest of us who live here. Speaking of sociological studies, one of the most memorable sights that I have seen during high season was a gentleman in white pants and white shoes sitting at a bar as happy as he could be with a huge smile on his face and an expression that said he was in heaven. He was buying drinks and being fawned over by three of the most beautiful girls that he had ever seen—except that they were men. I often wonder how the night ended for him.

Then you get guys like the poor tourist I once met who gets scammed into paying a 3,000-baht bar fine by his cab driver then brags about it and *still* uses the driver as his guide ('Sorry, meter no work'). You have to laugh.

Although it's really not that amusing because a few weeks ago I met friend of mine from America in Ko Samui. He's fallen in love with a pole swinger and is now sending her US$260 a month because 'they love each other' and he speaks to her every day on the phone. High season may not be so amusing after all.

So Much Money,
So Little Time

Was it Richard Pryor who once said that cocaine is God's way of telling you that you have too much money? Possibly the same thing could be said for Thailand: there's a lot of money floating around out there. That's really half the problem when you visit or retire in the Kingdom.

A fellow in Nai Harn, Phuket bought eight rai of land. He built ten houses and a hotel complex of twenty bungalows, all at the same time. He spent a lot of money. The man was only forty-nine years old and owned some kind of business in coin-operated vending machines or gambling slots in Finland. He had lots of non-taxable cash pouring in and he could not spend it all in his own country. Unfortunately only two years later his Thai wife called the police to claim that the man had keeled over and died at the dinner table from a heart attack. There was no investigation and the wife lived happily ever after on all that property with all those houses.

Before I met my friend Danny Rinn from America he was a wine salesman in the States. After visiting Thailand several times he thought that it would be wonderful to be able to live and work here. He had heard that you need a Thai partner to be allowed to go into business and he had just the right guy: a very helpful tour guide who he'd met while on vacation. The tour guide was so obliging that he'd arranged all of the necessary paperwork. Danny only had to sign his name—no matter that he couldn't read Thai. Anyway it had to be in Thai or it wouldn't be legal.

Danny spent four million baht importing a container of wine, and he and his new partner—who received twenty-five per cent of the company for his assistance—went about selling and distributing the merchandise. A year passed and the business was doing well until one day the police came and arrested Danny for not having a work permit. His partner had called them to get Danny out of the way. Danny finally saw a lawyer and showed him all the business papers. It turned out that even though his partner had told him he had a work permit, it was nowhere to be found. He also discovered that his partner owned seventy-five per cent of the business and Danny owned only twenty-five per cent.

'What! Do you believe that!' Danny exclaimed to his lawyer. 'I put up all of the money. How can he own seventy-five per cent?'

'Of course I believe it. It says it right here as plain as day.' The lawyer waved the papers at Danny.

Danny tried to salvage what he could by moving some of the wine from the warehouse to his home. His partner took him to court and sued him for theft. Danny had his passport taken away and went to jail until he could make bail. Four years later, after dragging the case through the courts, Danny was broke, had lost everything and still does not have his passport as his partner is appealing some of the court's decisions.

A few years ago a German restaurant opened on Viset Road in Rawai. The prospective operator offered top rent for the site, so much in fact that the landlord immediately threw out his present tenants who were managing a karaoke bar. The place was enlarged to hold 125 people. I thought that this was a huge amount of seats for a small town like Rawai. I found out later that the owner had a 2,000-seat restaurant in Munich, so I guess he didn't think that one with a mere 125 seats in Phuket was all that big.

The food was good but there were just not enough people to support a business that large and the place has been up for sale for months now. Same goes for the German beer garden that opened on a hill just above Patong. It got a nice write-up in the *Phuket*

Gazette. The owner boasted that he could serve between twenty and 400 people a night. He had 1,200 seats, a huge new kitchen and figured he could do two turnovers a night.

He's still waiting for the crowds to come.

Another American man here in Rawai was looking to buy or rent a house. He met two very pleasant Thai brothers who offered to build him a seriously nice house to his specifications. They gave him a thirty-year lease and a beautiful house for only five million baht. They were so accommodating that they also made sure all of the paperwork was done. The lease was signed and the American received his copy. Three years later the brothers knocked on the door with the police to evict him. The American had paid five million for only a three-year lease instead of a thirty-year lease. The case is still in court.

I have a friend who's an attorney for one of the largest law firms in Phuket. He was telling me about a man who came to see him. The man had bought a small resort, sight unseen, for US$40,000. He had what appeared to be all the proper paperwork, deeds and titles. When he went to claim ownership the people at the resort laughed at him. They had never heard of the man who had claimed to own the resort. There was nothing that my lawyer friend could accomplish on his client's behalf.

'Why do people do this?' I asked him.

'A person who comes here usually bought a house thirty or forty years ago for US$35,000 and sold it for US$600,000, plus he has his savings and pension plan. The people coming here have too much money. A guy comes here and his new girlfriend wants to open a beer bar for a million baht. That's small potatoes to him. It's like that old joke: How do you make a small fortune in Thailand? Come with a large fortune.'

I almost forgot to mention Gerald, my newly retired friend America. He lives in Patong and his girl wanted him to invest 50,000 baht in a travel and tourist stand.

'Thai people don't know the meaning of the word lend,' I

tried to dissuade him. 'They think it means give.'

Gerald did put up the money but took the precaution of getting a promissory note witnessed by two people. It sounded like a reasonable thing to do, but then again he hasn't been in Thailand that long. The next day the girl went home to Isaan and never came back. I reckon up there she can put her feet up and relax for a year on that kind of money.

Saa and Frank
Go to Ko Samui

'Can we go to Ko Samui?' said Saa, my housekeeper/companion.

'Why?'

'I want to see what it looks like.'

'Okay, go down to Nai Harn Beach. Walk on the sand and take a good look around and say: "I'm in Ko Samui." Then you will know what it looks like—same as here.'

Saa has been with me for the past six months, almost right off the cabbage truck from Roi Et, not counting the two months she put in at a local karaoke bar. She's twenty-two years old and has that sturdy build typical of girls from Isaan. Early in the morning, before I've even woken up, she's swept and mopped the floor, watered the plants and fed the three dogs and one cat. I'm next.

Her greatest concern seems to be what I am going to have for breakfast. I had to stop telling her because as soon as I stepped out of bed, my meal appeared. I like to take it easy in the morning, check my email, not eat too soon.

Saa could not speak a word of English so I sent her to school for three hours a week.

'What did you do before you came to Phuket?' I asked.

'I am farmer.' So I purchased half a dozen shrubs to plant in the yard and once I saw her wielding the shovel there was no doubt in my mind. I swear it reminded me of a chef reducing an onion to a stack of thin slices with a flick of his knife.

Saa traveled home a few months ago for two weeks to help her parents harvest the rice crop. Before I'd hired her she'd conveyed to me in her soft voice that this was non-negotiable. She had an obligation to go.

I received an email from my friend Billy who lives in New York City. He said he was going to spend the next three weeks in Ko Samui. On his last trip he'd fallen madly in like with a pole swinger. I'd been with him last year in Ko Samui but left a day before his fateful meeting. Since then he'd spent two weeks with her in Ko Samui during the summer and called her every day on the phone. Billy has spent a month every year in Southeast Asia for the past four years, so he is not really a newcomer to the bar scene. I usually hook up with him for a week or so: Patong, Bangkok, Bali, Cambodia. When we do go out at night to the bars and hear the usual cries of 'Handsome man', no one is speaking to me. I might as well be invisible.

Billy would be the last guy you would take with you if you wanted to pick up a girl. He's one of those tall, dark, and handsome types with a perpetual smile on his face. The go-go girls go ga-ga over him. I thought that his new girl must be one heck of a knockout. I was anxious to meet her.

'Saa, we are going to Ko Samui.'

'Really? Really?' she happily exclaimed in her soft voice.

I bought the tickets by telephone and we made arrangements for a friend to feed the animals while we were away.

'Will you be afraid to fly?' I asked Saa.

'I don't know.' A sensible answer, I thought.

We checked in at the counter and I picked up our boarding passes.

'Saa, the clerk wants you to step on the scale to make sure we are not overweight.'

'I don't think so,' she replied. It's one of her favorite responses if she doubts me.

Arriving in Samui I found that the cab drivers at Bangkok's

airport had nothing on the cabbies there. No one would put their meter on. Flat rates only. Six hundred baht from the airport and if you wanted to go out at night, it seemed to be 400 baht no matter where you went, then 400 baht to get back to your hotel. Almost made me wistful for the *tuk-tuk* drivers in Patong who charge 100 baht to go one or two blocks.

We were staying at a bungalow smack on the beach, relaxing on the porch, watching the waves roll in, when I saw Billy walking up the path. He seemed to have one of the older massage ladies in tow. Why, I couldn't work out. She had large teeth protruding from a constantly open mouth, and ears that stuck out like a car's side-view mirrors. After a big hug and a hello, he introduced me to his girl, Mutt. Billy is so tall, handsome and slim that I expected his girl to be a female version of him, not some old hooker with more miles on her than a used car. She had a loud grating voice and never stopped talking as Billy looked on admiringly.

Later we went out for dinner and Mutt talked so much I found myself turning away in my seat to keep my sanity. She spoke incessantly of wanting to meet Billy's mother and of getting married to Billy. Billy just sat there and smiled.

The next night, when we went to eat with a group of friends, Saa and I waited until Mutt had sat down before we grabbed the seats farthest away. After dinner we all went to a local bamboo bar. Mutt knocked back three tequilas and started dancing behind the bar with the other girls. Billy, still smiling, thought it was all quite entertaining while Saa and I discretely but desperately searched for one of those 400-baht cabs—an offer which was starting to look pretty good.

The following day Saa made it clear that she was not going to have dinner with us, no matter what.

'You can go. I stay here.'

'You have to eat. Please come with me.'

'No, Mutt talk too much.'

'What does she say?'

'Say work reception. I don't think so.'

'She does work reception. She accepts many bananas.'

'You speak not good. You go—go dinner, go bar, look ladies, I don't care. I not go. I stay here.'

I love my pal Billy but to tell you the truth his girl was also making me dizzy with her constant nonsensical chatter. We begged off for the evening and happily Billy came to visit me the next day for breakfast at the hotel. The restaurant was on the beach close by the pool. It was a lovely day; the sun was shining and there was a cool breeze. During our meal Billy confided in me that he was sending Mutt 10,000 baht a month. He also said he thought that he could retire in five years and Mutt wanted him to buy a house now; he could save money this way as houses certainly would be more expensive in five years' time and she would help with the details of the purchase. He could even pay it off by sending her monthly installments. Billy continued his story:

'Let me put it this way,' he told her. 'How much would it take for you to stop making boom-boom with other men?'

'Ten thousand baht a month,' she replied, claiming she was new to the game and had only been working at the bar for a few months, having learned near-perfect English working in a tailors (not by banging more *farang*s than there are coconuts in Samui).

Billy told me: 'She's going to keep on working in the bar but will not go with anyone else but me. I know this is true because I asked her girlfriend and she told me that Mutt does not go with anyone, she just stays at the bar and waits for me. She really loves me. Besides, we promised to always tell each other the truth. Now I can really trust her.'

Yeah, right, I thought. She's making a few thousand baht a night lying on her back for half an hour and she is going to give all that up and stay celibate because 'she loves you'. But all I managed to say was: 'Bill, have you ever checked out that website I told you about—Thailandnights.com?'

'No, why?'

'I think you would like it. It has many interesting stories about Thailand.'

Except I know that Bill does not read, not even a John Grisham paperback or a newspaper. He has an ipod and listens to music instead. Actually when I heard this I was speechless—dumbfounded. Guys from New York were supposed to be tough and smart. And this girl—woman, really—at forty years old (Billy is fifty)—had him wrapped around her little finger. I was at least expecting her to be a tall lithe young thing, then I would understand it better. After all, Jasmine Fever can strike anyone.

But would reading a website recounting tales of failed relationships do any good—really? I suppose not. A smack on the head with a baseball bat may not even help.

I was in a quandary; it was a difficult situation. What right did I have to tell my friend that the girl he loved was a scheming old whore. He would surely be angry and would resent my advice. After all, maybe she *was* a good girl who was telling the truth and they would live happily ever after. But then again, maybe I could teach pigs to whistle Dixie. Was it up to me to say?

I immediately called my pal MacDonald back in Phuket and told him the whole deal. What should I do? I told him the guy was a friend of mine. MacDonald is often my conscience and a guiding light in my stubborn and opinionated existence.

'Leave the man alone will you. If he's happy, he's happy.'

'I'm really concerned how this is going to turn out,' I said.

'Just keep your mouth shut and mind your own business.'

And so I did.

In the meantime Saa was having difficulties of her own.

'I miss dogs. They must be lonesome. I want go home.'

'You are the one that wanted to come here.'

'I know but I don't want to go away anymore. I want to stay home with the dogs.'

'So if I go away again, you don't want to come?'

'Yes.'

'You miss the dogs more than me? You love them more than me?'

Saa pondered this question for a minute.

'I love everyone but I want to stay with the dogs.'

Another diplomatic answer from my sweet girl.

Saa and Frank
Return From Ko Samui

No matter where you travel to it's always nice to go home. Our three dogs and one cat met us at the gate and jumped all over us. My big dog, Louke, was so happy he was crying, I swear. Saa and I sat down and gave them lots of hugs. There was some food shopping to do, mostly for them. We went to the open-air market and bought five kilos of chicken legs and four kilos of small fish. Saa boiled the fish and chicken separately, saved the fish water and gave it the plants.

When we got back I sat on the front porch, relaxing with a glass of wine, still thinking of my friend Billy who we'd visited in Ko Samui. Then my front gate opened and in came my pal Werner from Sweden. He stays three or four months every year and we always visit each other. Since he is a close friend I told him of my concerns about Billy and his bargirl. I'm worried about the guy.

'A cause to worry,' said Werner, 'because when they say that they will continue working in a bar but not make boom-boom with a man, it's not very likely.'

'You know, Saa and I were just about to come to your house and surprise you. Saa has a few girlfriends and I thought we would bring one over to you since your girl, Poot, has left.'

'Poot's back so it's just as well you didn't come to my house with another girl.'

'What? Again?' Werner met Poot last year and has been in touch with her ever since. He asked if he could bunk in with me for a while earlier this year while he looked for a house to rent so

I said yes, and who arrives with him but Poot. Okay, they were easy guests and found a house before too long. No problem. He gave Poot her month's salary in advance then she asked him for 3,000 baht so she could learn English. She just didn't mention she was going to learn English in Bangkok, and promptly took off with her cash in hand. A few weeks later she knocked on his window at three in the morning with no money and no place to stay—so she's back.

I had to break my friends balls and said, 'Wow, I bet her English has improved a lot by now.' Werner took it like a man and just shrugged his shoulders. The following week he advanced her 2,000 and she disappeared for another week.

Werner continued: 'She's looking for a job in an office in Bangkok so she doesn't have to go back to working in a bar when I leave. In the meantime she goes out most afternoons looking for a job here in Phuket. Sometimes she is so busy she has to sleep over with her sister.'

'What do you care? You have a wife at home anyway. What difference does it make?' I said. (Besides, I thought, Poot's as dumb as a table top and about as ambitious as a Barcalounger. She has about as much chance of getting a job in an office as my Springer Spaniel.)

'Well, that's just it. I'm going to get a divorce when I go home. It will be so much easier when I am a free man.'

'And then what?'

'Then I can come here for at least six months out of the year and live with Poot. We made a vow to always tell each other the truth, so now I trust her completely. She's not going to work in a bar anymore. Her sister told me so.' It was a good thing I was sitting down. Am I the only sane visitor here? What happens to these people? Am I hearing Billy's story all over again? I don't mean to be unkind and say that Poot would look more at home behind a plow. Actually she would look more natural pulling a plow rather than pushing it.

Later I told the story to Saa, my housekeeper. 'What do you think?' I asked her, because you know how Thai girls love to gossip. It's their main form of entertainment—that and mobile phones, sleeping at any time, or television soap operas where every female character is either screaming or crying. Saa knew the whole story. Poot was entertaining four men at the same time—mainly an Englishman and a Norwegian—along with Werner. She was a busy woman. Well, a girl's got to earn a living, as they say, and it is high season—make hay while the sun shines. Time will tell what happens to Billy and Werner, I thought. I'll just wait and see.

But I have an even better story to tell. You can't make these things up. Werner told me about his two friends, a married couple also from Sweden. They have odd-sounding names, to me anyway. Names that sound like Fin and Fan. They have been coming here for three months every high season for the past nine years, so they are not newcomers to the Land of Smiles. Fin and Fan thought it would be nice to own a bar—make some money and have an income even when they weren't in Thailand. They found an empty store in a small hotel, newly built, between Kata and Karon, on a back road. Not an auspicious location, I thought. They paid 75,000 baht as key money. (What? 75,000 baht as key money for an empty store?) They bought a bar, a fridge, a stove, some tables, chairs and so forth, all costing another 100,000 baht. They are also paying 35,000 baht a month to rent a property in a location that calls for no more than 12,000 or 15,000 at the most. They will be here for only three months out of the year but have solved that problem by paying the hotel owner 4,000 a month to watch over the bar in their absence.

No doubt they expect a tidy profit on their return, having told their new manager to obtain receipts for any liquor he buys, and to keep all the bar checks as they are numbered in order.

There, that should insure success—Ha!

It's a wonderland here in Thailand. The Thais are wonderfully

165

happy and so are the foolish *farang*s.
    And me? I just sit back and wonder.

Thai Girls and
Nigerian Guys

I was just talking to a friend of mine who lives and works as a school teacher in Bangkok. He emailed me a note he had received from a Thai girl that he knows. In it she tells him that her employer has passed away and has left her 400,000 baht. She needs to borrow 200,000 in order to pay the taxes and hire a lawyer, and she will return his money in a few weeks. A little too ambitious and far-fetched but I have no doubt that she will eventually refine her request until it sounds almost believable.

What I found absolutely fascinating is that her story reminds me of a Nigerian letter scam. I don't think I need to explain the scheme here. We have all heard about it and it has been documented many times in Trink's old column in the *Bangkok Post* newspaper.

My friend in Bangkok said, 'Just think, if one Thai girl catches onto this, soon they'll all be offering a cash profit along with a warm body. But will anyone actually fall for this?'

I think they will. And the thing about it is that a convoluted story is not really necessary. There are so many expats and visitors here willing—even anxious—to part with their cash. Why is this I wondered? It's a double whammy with the girl asking for money and the guy wanting to give it away. I think it's a matter of self-esteem. A guy comes here, middle-aged or older, divorced, hasn't had a date in ten years, feels more comfortable drinking beer with his buddies than socializing in mixed company or talking to a woman. He's not in the best of shape, cannot be called good-looking by any means, hasn't gone out with an attractive girl in forty years, if ever. And now, all of a sudden, a firm-bodied twenty-two-year-old honey is calling him handsome man and pledging her eternal love. Does this make him feel better? No, it makes him feel worse, even more insecure.

'I'm just some old schlep,' he's thinking. 'What is this girl doing with me?'

So what does he do? He compensates. He wants to feel more confident, like he's a worthy man, a man in charge of his life, a man his girl can look up to and depend on. A man willing to reach out and help this young beauty who has fallen for him and also a girl that may wake up and leave at any moment. How to keep her interested? How to keep her? Easy. Step up to the plate and act like a man. Put your money where your mouth is.

Minutes after I spoke to my friend in Bangkok I was visited by a casual acquaintance called Craig. It took him about an hour of chit-chat to tell me why he'd come. He wanted to show me a text message on his phone and ask my advice. Craig has been living in Thailand for ten years and is a Hash House Harrier. During a run in Phuket he met a Filipino girl serving lunch to the runners. They started to date and go out with her sister and her Thai boyfriend. No boom-boom, only friends. She told him that her brother back home was in the hospital and she needed 10,000 baht to get him out. Craig gave her the money and didn't hear from her for the next few weeks. Then he received a phone message that she was in the Philippines and wanted to return to Thailand and live with him, if he could just send her the money for a plane ticket.

'Please deposit the money in my bank account at Siam Commercial,' she said. He did and waited for her to fly into his arms. Her arrival date came and went without a word. A few weeks later he got another text message. She had been delayed and needed another 10,000 to allow her to leave the country.

His question to me is: 'Shall I send her the money?'

'Sit down here,' I replied. 'I'm going to get a bucket of ice water. I'll be right back.'

'What?'

My first thought was to scold him. Christ, he should know better. What an idiot. But something came over me. All of a sudden I felt very sorry for the man.

Oddly enough, he is normally a very tight-fisted guy. He leaves tips of only five and ten baht at restaurants and won't even pay for bottled water. He has had two different girls living with him but after refusing to spend very much on them, they left. I sat down and tried to explain things to him.

'Craig, you know you can't give girls money just like that. How do you even know she's even in the Philippines? She may be living around the corner sending the same message to a dozen guys.' He slowly saw the light and went home, a sadder but wiser man.

I called my friend in Bangkok. 'You won't believe what just happened. Exactly what we were talking about. Guys giving away money at the drop of a hat.'

Speed Dating

When I lived in American in the 1980s and 1990s, personal advertisements were popular. I put more than my fair share in *New York Magazine*. The cost was about US$160, including a box number at the magazine from which they would forward your mail to you every week. I met some nice girls that way. I also met girls that were looking for their own special Prince Charming; someone rich and handsome with a great job like investment banker or CEO of their own company, guys with the ability to take them on luxurious vacations and shower them with presents. I didn't have much luck with these women. I know that these days, in the age of the Internet and online dating, everyone is using the computer to make personal connections, to find a partner, a lover. But eventually it comes down to that face-to-face meeting—which is a good thing because, after all, that's what we're looking for. In fact, we're looking for a good deal more than that, aren't we?

I was thinking how much easier it is to date here in Thailand—for us men anyway. Speed dating is the new answer to the personals. And living in Thailand is the new answer to speed dating.

Speed dating is an interesting concept. An agency arranges a meeting of men and women, usually in groups ranging from twelve to twenty of each sex. You receive a list of everyone's name with a box marked 'yes' or 'no' next to it. The women sit at tables or in booths, usually in a restaurant, and each man spends four minutes with each lady. The men move along, like in a game of musical chairs. There are no awkward moments such as asking a girl for her phone number. All you do is check the boxes. The women do the same, and later the organizers review the data and if two people have checked 'yes' and there's a match you have a date. It's a lot like going to Rainbow Two in Nana Plaza, except that there you have hundreds of girls to choose from instead of just a dozen, and they sit down with you rather than you moving from girl to girl. At Rainbow the time you have with each girl is about the same—about four minutes. That's how long you have to decide. After four minutes, or sometimes sooner, they say, 'You pay bar.' If you haven't made a decision when your time is up they simply move along to the next man—speed dating at its fastest.

The girls at Rainbow Two are earners and do not have time for idle chit-chat. You'll have more time to decide who will be the girl of your

if you go to an outdoor beer bar in Phuket or Pattaya. The girls there are obligated to stay at that location, and the bars are usually not that big so you can take a while with the conversation and getting-to-know-you time.

Usually one has to pay a fee to join a speed-dating club. It's a little more than the amount of a bar fine in Bangkok. The speed-dating fee can be compared to buying girly drinks in a go-go bar. The cost of taking a girl home from a bar in Thailand is less than taking a 'speed date'out to dinner, and the end result is guaranteed. I leave it to you to decide which is the best option.

There are other similarities here too. Of course women prefer young handsome men, but a study of more than 20,000 online daters found that it's just as easy for a five-foot-five man to obtain a date as it is for a six-foot-tall, man as long as he makes more money. A bald, five-foot-tall man can come by a date effortlessly if he makes a great deal of money. This is similar to when you are sitting in a Nana Plaza bar with a real cutie ensconced on your lap and you are about to close the deal when a group of Japanese men walk in. What happens? The girl jumps off your lap as if she was sitting on a hot stove and runs over to the Japanese guys—simple arithmetic.

If you really have a desire for a certain girl and she doesn't appear that interested in you, you're probably better off letting her go as later she will turn into a starfish, just Cinderella's coach turned into a pumpkin.

But if you are a short, bald man you can stir her interest in a few ways. You can say that you have just arrived today and have never been to Thailand (you will almost hear the cash register ringing in her head). Or you can say you are staying at the Hilton or J. W. Marriott. If you do get her back to your 500-baht bungalow just say, 'Hilton full tonight. Stay there tomorrow night.' Or if you really want to impress her just say the magic words: 5,000 baht, short time. That usually does the trick.

What about all those lithe beauties filling up the sky train and mobbing the streets and shopping malls with their short skirts and long hair? Do you have a chance to date them? Sure, if you are young and handsome, no problem. If you are not, there are a few things that you can do if you want to have a better chance at accosting girls on the street or in the shopping centers. Go to the Emporium on Sukhumvit Road and buy an expensive suit along with a few shirts, ties, and a briefcase too, even if you don't have a job. A friend of mine in New York City always carried a huge roll of blueprints under his arm, print side out. It looked impressive. A good suit is even more awe-inspiring here in Thailand, where looks and appearance are valued. Shopping malls, such as the new Siam Center, are always great places to find prospective dates. But stay away from the cosmetic counters where the girls are all beautiful but half of them are girls/boys.

If you are asked what you do and don't have a job or are retired, do what I do and say you are in banking or that you own a business and employ forty-five people. Doesn't matter what you say; when did a Thai girl ever tell you the truth anyway? What's amazing to me is that when a guy comes here, all of a sudden he turns fussy. Here's a guy who hasn't had a date in twelve years and back home could not pick up a girl with a shovel. But suddenly here he is picky and particular. I think it's the wealth of possibilities that does it—with all those girls to choose from, one starts striving for perfection. I went out for a drink with a friend of mine and he squeezed the arm of every girl that he spoke to, squeezed them as if they were grapefruit in a supermarket.

'What are you doing that for?' I asked.

'It's a test. If their arm is soft it means that they have had a baby and, who knows, their stomach may be full of hash marks. If their arm is firm, odds are their entire body is firm and they do not have any kids.' This from a guy who couldn't get the time of day from a girl back home.

A study on dating from the University of Chicago says that: 'Humans have a highly attuned ability to assess such subtleties as romantic attraction. It's the need to feel special, unique or loved that stretches across people's social lives.'

Did they really need a study to find that out? All they had to do was to come here for a day and watch a bargirl at work. The way she puts her arm around a guy, looks into his eyes, and holds him close, pressing up against him, all in the space of a few minutes after he sits down at the bar. Talk about romantic attraction. If the guy is not attracted by then, he's dead.

Thai girls don't need studies, psychological profiles, study groups, or dating tips. They are naturally instinctive, and even though they may not be highly educated they are a lot smarter than many of the visitors that come here. Many of my friends don't want to come with me when I go to Soi Bangla in Patong. They just want to sit at a bar, have a drink and relax, but I have a drink in half a dozen bars, hardly finishing the drink, moving along, speaking to as many girls as possible.

It's my own version of speed dating, right here in Phuket.

A Trip to Cambodia

It was time to go to Cambodia. I had not seen my friend Jake for a year and my pal Michael was arriving from New York City. Every year Michael spends a week in Phuket then two weeks in Pattaya. He has been doing this for the past twelve years. He always stays at the Safari Hotel on the beach road, a block in from Soi Bangla, and insists on room 214. If he has to he will settle for room 213 or 215. To say he is a creature of habit would be putting it mildly. I had been asking him to come to Cambodia with me for years and I was surprised when he said he wanted to see Angkor Wat. I readily agreed to accompany him and arranged to be on the same flight from Bangkok when he traveled up from Pattaya. Mike was going to sacrifice a week's stay in Pattaya and find some culture instead of the same old girly bars. Michael does not date in NYC and hardly ventures out for dinner. The city has become far too expensive. Instead he saves his money for an annual trip to Southeast Asia.

I have to say that I was concerned about our Cambodia trip as Michael is usually quite rigid in his schedule: breakfast at ten, then to the internet shop, lunch at two, and to the beach at precisely three. Dinner in the exact same restaurant every night then to a beer bar or two for a club soda.

Luckily things worked out perfectly. Jake picked us up at Phnom Penh's airport in his four-wheel drive. I was splashing out with a stay at Hotel Cambodiana as Mike was going up to Siem Reap for a few days and I wanted to relax by the pool. Mike was staying at Flamingos Hotel, a stone's throw from Shanghai Bar and Walkabout. We decided we would drop Mike off first then pick him up later and go out for dinner as it was already eight o'clock in the evening.

On the way from the airport Mike said that his friends told him not to go to Cambodia as it might be dangerous. Just as Jake and I both replied, 'Don't be silly!', we hit a traffic jam. Something was blocking the road ahead. It was a body, sprawled out on the street, about a quart of fresh blood surrounding the head. The police had already chalked an outline around the man. We passed just as an ambulance came by—but it was too late. The traffic was fierce. There were plenty of motorbikes, most with their lights off, crowding the dark streets. Ahead of us two guys on a bike kicked another bike passing next to them and the driver fell to the ground. The passenger jumped off and immediately began beating the fallen boy with a chain. Jake jammed his car in front of the still-standing bike and jumped out. As the guy with the chain turned, Jake gave him a hard shove in the chest with both hands and the kid flew back into the air. The kid scrambled to his feet in one motion, jumped onto the back of the bike, and the two guys took off. The fallen rider also left the scene and we continued on to Mike's hotel.

'What happened ?' I asked.

'Just a couple of wise-guy punks.'

We approached Flamingos Hotel from an unpaved side street filled with ruts, stones, and no street lights.

'Can I walk around here?' Mike asked in a tone that really meant: 'I can't believe that I came to Cambodia.'

'Stay on the main street and don't go too far,' I said. I dropped my bag off Hotel Cambodiana. It was once the grandest place in town but now is so out-classed by the newer fancier hotels springing up that it has had to lower its prices.

Jake and I had a surprise in store for Michael, one that has given us great fun for three years in a row with different friends. We ate dinner in an exquisite open-air French restaurant that Jake picked out, then went on to the famous Sharky's Bar.

'First we must stop and run in for just a second to see a friend,'

I told Mike.

Le Cyrcee Club is a dump of a bar situated on an unpaved dark street with a curtained door and windows. Just the kind of place a casual visitor would give a wide birth. The dimly lit room was so narrow that you could touch the bar and the opposite wall at the same time. I walked in first and a dozen scantily clad girls rushed toward us. I waved my contingent towards Michael who barely had time to get situated on a stool before he was overrun with cute girls. Two sat on each knee while four stood on the rungs of his stool and clambered all over him, hugging, hanging on, caressing him, and cooing in his ear. Eight pretty girls vied for his attention at the same time. Unlike the bargirls in Thailand, none of the young ladies asked for a drink.

After five minutes one of them whispered in Michael's ear, 'You go upstairs with me?'

'What's the deal here?' Michael asked and I knew that he had heard the magic words. I personally defy any man to say no after this kind of welcome. Even Superman would find one of these beauties hard to resist. There were four rooms upstairs and they were all full; Michael would have to wait another day.

We drove down to Sharky's, a large second-floor bar with pool tables, and filled with Vietnamese and Khmer freelancers. No trip to Phnom Penh is complete without a visit to Martini Bar so we gave moved on there and gave Michael the grand tour. He was amazed to notice that not one girl had a tattoo, unlike Pattaya where the girls wear them like a badge of honor.

The next day was a treat for me; we visited a new branch of Friends Restaurant. The chain is run by a woman who teaches street children about the restaurant business through hiring them in her eateries. We ate lunch at Romdeng Restaurant on street number 278, behind the Lucky Market. It wasn't far from the Independence Monument where, in the early evening, dozens of girls can be seen lounging on the grass waiting for customers. I opened the menu that boasted a taste of the provinces and saw what I was looking for: crispy tarantulas served with lime and pepper sauce. The menu went on to explain that the spiders come from the town of Skun in Kampong Cham.

'I know what I'm having,' I exclaimed.

Jake chimed in: 'I haven't seen you so happy since you ate those grilled snakes in Siem Reap. You'd eat the north end of an animal going south if it was on the menu.'

Michael was looking at the fish stew with tomatoes and galangal.

'What's galangal?'

'It's like fresh young ginger,' I said.

'You know, like the girl on *Gilligan's Island* before the professor and the skipper get hold of her,' says Jake.

We also ordered grilled pork fillet stuffed with toasted coconut, and grilled eggplant with pork and coriander.

The spiders had the texture of popcorn and the accompanying sauce was tasty. The legs were a bit scratchy to eat and they didn't have much meat on them. My housekeeper from Roi Et says arachnids taste much better if they have eggs inside of them.

We also ate in a superb Spanish restaurant called Pacharan Tapas & Bodega. It's situated on the second floor with a view of the river and the Royal Palace. Excellent wine list, great food, and reasonable prices. In Phnom Penh there are so many good French restaurants with affordable prices it makes Phuket look like a backwater small town. If you are interested in good food and wine, Phnom Penh is certainly worth a visit.

I'm Not
Complaining But ...

I want to have a weekly column in *The Nation* like Roger Beaumont has and the words above will be the title. Every week I will grumble about something or other and, of course, it will do not one bit of good and nothing will change.

This week's topic will be about the concept of service here in Thailand. Service is defined as 'the action of helping or doing work for someone'. Now I bet you think a restaurant rant is coming up. You're wrong. I'm going to do that next week, talk about all those vacant-eyed waiters on the floor when the place is jam-packed and full to the rafters. They, on the other hand, are on the same speed as when the place was almost empty—that is from stop to slow to zombie.

This week I do want to complain about service but we have to narrow it down a bit. And every time I complain about a topic I will offer a workable solution to the problem. 'Yeah, right.' Okay, all I can do is make a few suggestions.

I was sitting at home the other day. Rain in Rawai and a few drinks is always a dangerous combination as all kinds of thoughts creep into your head. It's off season and I was bored out of my skull. The phone rang and it was some bargirl from Kata who I'd taken home a year before. She was probably as bored silly as I was and, since my name begins with a V, I suspected that she had already worked through her entire phone book trying to drum up some moron to keep her company on such a dreary day and I was the end of the line. So I figured why not, jumped into my car, and

185

went over to pick her up. Oddly enough she lives right next door to Kata Wat, and I mean right next door—you have to drive into the grounds to get to her apartment. We were almost to my house when she asked, 'Are you hungry?'

Well, it was about two in the afternoon and we were just passing my favorite Thai restaurant, a humble thatched-roof affair with excellent food. I pulled over and turned off the ignition.

'The food here is no good. I want to go to the beach and eat seafood.'

'It's raining now. It will be windy and wet,' I replied. What I was actually thinking was: if you believe that I'm going to buy you a shrimp dinner and let you eat as if it's your last meal, you're crazy.

'I'm not going to the beach,' I said. 'Do you want to eat here or not?'

'No.'

I started the car and drove home. Once in my house she asked for a glass of red wine. Okay, no problem.

'Do you have any cocaine? No? How about some grass? Let's get some. I'll call my friend and have it delivered.'

'No thanks, I don't do that,' I replied. 'Let's just stick to the program.' Christ, what was she going to ask for next?

It didn't take her long. We started to take a shower and I suggested that she have a smoke.

'That's going to be 2,000 then.'

'No way. We agreed on 1,000 and, besides, you always smoke so cut the crap.'

'I need the money for my baby.'

'You don't have a baby.'

'I mean my sister's baby. She's sick.' Then I was beyond annoyed. 'Do you want to grab a towel and dry off and I'll take you home?'

'No, no, I was just asking.'

Later, when it was over and we were getting ready to leave, I pressed a 1,000-baht bill into her hand.

'How about a tip?'

'For what?'

'I always ask for a tip.'

'Yes, but we agreed on 1,000 and you didn't do anything special.'

'Don't be a cheapskate,' she said as she held up all five fingers on her right hand, firmly clutching the silver note with her other hand.

'Five-hundred-baht tip? You're losing your mind. Let's go.'

The little Thai restaurant wasn't far away and as we approached it she said, 'Let's stop here and eat.'

'We can't. You said the food is no good.'

'But I'm hungry now.'

I just kept on driving.

'Okay, then give me some money for food and I'll eat later.'

'Sure, that's no problem. I just gave you 1,000 baht. You can eat for a week on that, or call up ten girl friends and take them all out for dinner tonight.'

I took her home and dropped her off. On the way back I was thinking what a ball-busting experience that was.

That's the last time for her. And the most amazing part about the whole thing? She showed up at my door a few nights later with her motorbike. She wanted to come in and 'hang out for a while'. She thought that her greedy money-grubbing ways were perfectly normal. Now that's really no way to behave. The first rule of business is that you must be of service to your customer—and I mean really be of service, not just go through the motions.

It's always risky to take a bargirl home. Eight times out of ten it's simply not a very satisfying experience. I don't even want to do this anymore. And the prettier they are, the higher the chances that they will be lethargic and indolent. Do they think that they are so gorgeous that all they have to do is lie there?

Now here's the solution that I promised.

I am going to have some cards printed up, about the size of a business card or a bit larger. One side will be in Thai and the other in English so if the girl can't read or doesn't understand, someone may be able to explain it to her. The first rule in any presentation, as in business, is to put the other person first, make it interesting to them right from the start. The message would begin something like this:

'How would you like to have a very profitable business and make money every day? You can have customers all the time and without sitting in a boring beer bar every night staring into space. The key to your success here is repeat business. Repeat business is when you have customers coming back time after time. You must treat your customer with care and do as good of a job as is possible. You have to spend the next half an hour with the man, no matter how you look at it. Why not show him the best time that you can? And then he may bar-fine you out a second time or call you again.

'If you treat everyone nicely and give them good value for their money instead of being lazy and remiss in your duties, they may call you again and you can build up a list of clients that will call you back. You might establish a list of ten or twenty clients that you could count on every week—money in the bank.

'You probably have never been bar-fined out twice by the same person because you are too stupid and lackadaisical to be of use to anyone. As for me, you will never see me again because you did a terrible job, were no good and were not worth my time or my money. However I leave you this card as a tip. Pay attention.'

I put that last part in as I would only give this card to a girl who needed it—and most of them do.

If she was a nice girl and did a good job, then I would be handing her a real tip instead.

Stay tuned for next week's grumble.

Laos Lazy Days/Daze

I was sitting by myself at an open-air beer garden on the Mekong River in Vientiane, Laos, drinking a two-dollar pitcher of home-made beer. A soft breeze floated through the air as I gazed at Thailand just across the way. I had it in my mind that in a few days I would take a boat up river to Luang Prabang. Right now I was just relaxing, and the river was moving slowly with only a few boats drifting by. It was a lovely way to spend the afternoon.

Two attractive local girls sat down a few tables away and I looked for the waitress to send them over a drink. I should have got myself up off my rear end and gone over but it was just one of those laid-back days. A nice-looking young backpacker sat down at their table and started talking animatedly to them. They were receptive and everyone looked happy. There was an extra girl at the table but I felt it would have been intrusive to insert myself into this small scene.

Actually I wanted one of the girls, the taller one with the milk-white skin. They were both in their early twenties and the boy not much older; I had an idea what was going to happen, although I would probably never know for sure.

An hour or two went by and the three of them had left. I ordered another pitcher of beer and watched the light change on the river, the sky turning to an abstract panoply of serene purples and pastel orange. In my opinion the capital of Laos had superb French restaurants, even if the place was only a small town, and the wine prices were as gentle as the people. I wanted to linger a while, take my time and sample as many meals as I could.

I strolled over to an establishment that I had heard about and ordered a bottle of wine. As the waiter was opening a crisp, cold Sancerre, I glanced around and there, two tables away, was the trio that I had been observing at the riverside. The boy was paying the check and had obviously treated them to dinner. I don't know what his daily budget was but he'd done the right thing. I imagined that he thought he was on a date, just like back home. He was good-looking and picking up girls was, no doubt, not a problem for him. But this wasn't Ohio or Kansas or wherever it was that he came from.

By now I was a shameless voyeur, straining to hear every word. But they were so intent on their conversation that they never even noticed me.

'I want you to come back to my hotel with me ...' He was speaking to the taller girl.

'Yes.'

'Wonderful, let's go.'

'That's US$100.'

'What?' The young man was stunned, confused and surprised, all at the same time.

'You said you loved me.'

'I do.'

'I thought we were having a great time together.'

'We are.'

'And you want me to pay you?'

'Yes.'

The boy pushed his chair back and stormed out, the girls angrily shouting after him. They had wasted half of their evening, all to no avail. Of course, asking a hundred bucks was a bit over the top. After they calmed down somewhat I waved them over to my table.

'You want a drink?'

The taller girl rested her hand on my shoulder. 'Yes, but let's go down the street.' Okay, that was understandable after all the fuss. It turned out to be a nice bar and a bit romantic, with low-level lighting and soft banquets. We ordered three drinks and I took the time to have a good close-up look at the girls. They were both truly pretty and the shorter one was really beautiful. She knew only three words of English but they were good ones. She kept repeating them over and over to me, sitting back, looking directly at me, saying the same thing again and again, moving closer to whisper softly and sincerely in my ear, 'I love you. I love you.'

After a few drinks and listening to these enticing words, who could resist? Now it was my turn.

'You come back to my hotel with me?'

'One hundred dollars.'

I stood up to reach into my shoulder bag for a paper and pencil and they grabbed onto me as if I were a life jacket and they were on a sinking ship.

'Don't go.'

'I'm not leaving.' I was just trying to explain something to them. I wrote the number twenty on one piece of paper and the number zero on another piece. I put one in each hand and held them out.

'Which one do you want tonight?' I asked. They came to their senses and I ended up taking the smaller one back to my hotel. Since I had initially made eye contact with the taller girl first, she flared up and kicked over a chair on the way out. That left me with the girl who could only say, 'I love you'. And she kept on saying it. It was kind of nice really.

I'd had quite a lot to drink throughout the night but, as always, I remembered to take my wallet out of my pants and slip it underneath the mattress when the girl went to the bathroom. This time I was carrying my money belt, passport and all kinds of valuables, so I just folded up my pants and shoved everything underneath the bed. We made love and fell asleep. Sometime during the night she wanted to go home and I let her out.

Having a bit of a hangover the next day, I got up and took a shower, then looked for my pants. They were nowhere to be found.

I slumped down on a chair with my head in my hands and thought, 'She took my pants, I am really f**ked now.'

No pants or passport, no money or credit card. A palpable feeling of sheer despair engulfed me. I sat there in utter depression for a few minutes before I remembered that I had put my pants under the mattress.

I guess that momentary stupidity can strike anyone, not just backpackers.

The Disappeared

Saa, my housekeeper/companion, had lived with me for over a year. Her biggest concern was what I would have for breakfast every day. She wanted to have it ready when I woke up. She would feed my four dogs first and then bring my meal on a tray into the television room. She was sweet and considerate. She wanted to learn English so I sent her to school. Then she wanted to go to sewing school. I paid for that and bought her a sewing machine. She never went out at night.

When I took her to Ko Samui for a few days she missed the dogs and said she really did not want to go anywhere again. She had come down from Roi Et to be able to send some money home and was working in a Thai karaoke bar for about a month before we met. She seemed quite content to stay at my house and care for the dogs when I had to make the occasional trip to Bangkok. I paid her a few thousand baht more than the job called for, and everyone was happy.

I am planning a long trip in a year or two and she said she would be willing to take the dogs back to Roi Et and take care of them there. I told her money would not be a problem and that I would leave her with more than enough. I can only suppose that I did not leave soon enough to fit in with her goals.

I eat brunch with my lady friend Jules every Saturday. One Saturday Saa said she would go shopping with her girlfriend. Well, she never came home. I was up all day and night worrying that Saa had been in a motorcycle accident. I kept calling her phone but no answer. I took three sleeping pills, had two drinks and went to bed. I woke up the next day and still no Saa. I sat around in the morning wondering when she would show up. I know that sometimes the girls forget what time it is and really stay out late. I thought that later I would go to the Thai general hospital to see if she was dead or alive. David, one of my friends, visited me so I told him what had happend.

'Did you look to see if her clothes are missing?' he suggested.

Well, I hadn't even thought of that as there were some shirts and a few of her belongings lying around. So I looked in the closets and, yes, her clothes were gone! Frank, I thought, wake up and welcome to Thailand. She would've known that I have breakfast with Jules every Saturday for about two hours so she had plenty of time to pack. I was more baffled than anything. I guess she just felt like moving on and you know how Thais hate confrontation. So I reckon that she just packed up and left. She also absconded with my new leather bag. I can only be happy that she did not back up a truck to the front door and take the sewing machine and God knows what else.

The point is that I have lived here for almost ten years now, have had girls on and off like running water, and yet I simply had no inkling of what was about to happen. I'm still surprised at my naivety. I told a friend and he laughed out loud at me mentioning my missing bag. 'Be glad it wasn't your house.'

Well, that really grounded me, brought me back to earth. What was I worried about? A measly 6,000-baht bag. It's not like it was a gold necklace, is it? Could this be good for a short story? No, not really. No fights, quarrels or arguments. No gold necklaces. Wait! Possibly that was it. No gold forthcoming. No, she never asked for anything like that.

It's like the staff that I had back home. When they found a better position they simply never showed up for work. They did show up on payday. Then I had the pleasure of saying, 'Golly, I thought you were dead. Sorry, I never made out your check. Come back tomorrow.'

However Saa was wise enough to leave the Saturday after

she'd been paid her monthly salary. The only thing that has turned in my favor is that it's off season. Not much happening. So I decided that I could do without a housekeeper and it would be good for me to have some mild exercise. So I started doing a bit of cleaning every day.

Owoo was staying with her aunt in Kata when I ran into her. Her mother had told her to go to Phuket and send back some cash. She was much too cute to pass up and I knew she would not be walking around by herself for very long, low season or not. Twenty years old and adorable. On a scale from one to ten she's a twelve. She has been great the past week and is sweet as pie. However, I figure that when high season comes or when some girl tells her that she can make as much in half an hour as I am paying her in a week, she too will be among the disappeared.

Speaking of 'the missing', do you ever wonder what happened to all these Thai girls? Like the one you saw at the bar and went back to visit the next night but she was gone. You live here and you've never seen her since. They are all so transient, hopping from bar to bar, from place to place, then you never see them again. Where do they go? What happens to them? Do they all go to Singapore and Japan to work? Or do they get married and go to England and Europe? Do they grab a expatriate that has some cash and go back to live happily ever after in Isaan? Sure, and sometimes it's not them that's missing—it's you. Yes, they stay at 'their' house with 'their' appliances, jewelry and car.

And you're out. Get lost, you *farang* loser. Possibly one could put homing devices on a few of the really spectacular-looking girls. You know, shoot them with a dart or a tag like they do with dolphins or tigers. It would be an interesting study, wouldn't it? It could be a good story, like the ones you see on the National Geographic channel. Don't worry about the plain-looking ones— as they get older they all end up in massage parlors or the German beer garden on Soi Seven. You could track the pretty ones as if they were migratory birds, find out where they go. Perhaps shark tagging would be a better analogy. This would make another wonderful TV series if we could trail these beautiful but dangerous creatures as they hunt for their next conquest. Trace them from country to country as they stalk their prey, leaving a trail of broken hearts and empty bank balances behind.

Or like in the movie *Casino Royale*, when James Bond has a GPS homing device shot into his arm. Suppose you could do this to your girl when she is sleeping—shoot her behind the ear or in the rear end, go back to Europe and, as you are depositing thousands of baht into her account each month, you open your laptop and see where she really is, back home on the farm picking rice as promised, taking care of her mom and the buffalos. Hmm, you're tuning in—is it Ubon or Nakhon that's coming up? No, it's ... yes, by God, it looks like ... Walking Street in Pattaya. Jeez, who would have thought?

Looking for Love in All the Wrong Places

I passed the advertisement a few times. It looked liked all the other ones tacked to the wall of the grocery store. Visa runs, tours and travel, marriage applications, matchmaking for the handicapped.

Wait a minute. Matchmaking for the handicapped? I called the number. The office was in Karon. I would be right over. This might work, I reasoned. After all, if some girl is willing to go out with a handicapped person, why wouldn't she go out with me? A beat-up, sixty-year-old expatriate. This was my chance to find true love.

The name of the service was Deafeagle and, yes, the white guy behind the desk was hearing impaired. He pointed me towards his Thai assistant, an attractive young lady. I told her my reason for coming and she pulled out a neat-looking photo album and slid it over to me. She explained that the cost for membership would be 6,000 baht and that it was lifetime membership. I could find dates here for as long as I lived.

I opened it to see pictures of about forty girls with a little biography next to each one. Most of the girls stated that they would not mind going out with a deaf or disabled man.

The girls in the album were quite attractive. Golly, this looked good. I had plenty of time. Lifelong membership, I mused. Wonderful. I imagined an endless procession of nubile young ladies. I chose five beauties that I wanted to date. The girl explained to me that they would meet me there at the office.

'That will be 6,000 baht, please.' Wow, this seemed too good to be true.

'Can you just please check to see if they all are available?'

'Yes, that will be 6,000 baht, please.'

'I'll come back tomorrow and you let me know.'

'Can you give me 6,000 baht, please?'

'Tomorrow.'

I went back the next day. She could not get in touch with any of the ladies.

'When was the last time you spoke to any of them?'

'Last year.'

'Haven't you had any customers since last year?'

'We never had any customers for the matchmaking service. You are the first one. Tomorrow I will call more girls for you. Can you give me 6,000 baht, please?'

'I'll come back tomorrow.'

The next day she had five photos picked out from the album and she placed them in front of me.

'Six thousand baht, please.'

I perused my future companions. There were some attractive ones there. Their biographies said that they would accept a man up to the age of forty-five years old. I mentioned this to the girl.

'How old are you?'

'Sixty. These girls won't go out with me.'

There was one photo left. The poor old battleaxe was twice my size. The girl slid the photo towards me.

'I don't want to go out with her.'

'Why not?'

'She's too old.'

'You are old man. Why you no go out with old lady?'

'I may be old but I'm not stupid.'

'I find more ladies for you. Give me 6,000 baht, please. You can use this service long time'

'I can't use it if you have no ladies for me.' I gave up on this idea and drove towards my house, through Karon and Kata. It was quiet. Songkhran was over and many girls had headed home. The girly bars were, for the most part, uninhabited. Patong was just too far away. It took forty minutes to drive there and forty minutes to get back. If I took a girl home I would have to repeat the trip the next morning.

Maybe I could have a girl come to my house. But how? I asked Google. They seem to have the answer for everything. Up popped the names of a few dating services. Thailovelinks.com seemed like the best choice. For a mere US$27 a month I could contact hundreds of girls. I paid by credit card and started sending emails. Romance, here I come.

Half of the women on the site were almost as old as I was. That ruled them out. A quarter of them were really beautiful but only wanted young guys. I would find my beloved among the other twenty-five per cent. I was sure of it.

When I logged onto Hotmail in the mornings, there it was in bold print: SOMEONE IS INTERESTED IN YOU AT THAILOVELINKS. Great. I couldn't wait for each morning to come so that I could read the new messages. Many came from Khon Kaen and Udon Thani. But could they really read and write English this well? I didn't think so. It was too far to go anyway. I directed my attention to the girls in Bangkok. One girl looked terrific and I arranged to meet her since I travel to Bangkok once a month. She came to my hotel on Sukhumvit. She was at least ten years older than her photo and spoke very little English.

Another dead end.

I arranged to meet one more girl when I was there. She was a raving beauty and worked in a Japanese club. I met her in the lobby of my hotel. After I introduced myself, she put her arms around me and held me close. Not bad, I thought. This is going to be marvelous. She put her lips next to my ear and whispered to me: 'Short time, 3,000 baht.' Gee, that was not exactly the kind of true love that I had envisioned.

One email claimed to be from a Thai girl stranded in Nigeria. She had been part of a dance troupe but got left behind. They had paid her US$3,000 by cheque which, unfortunately, could only be cashed by her in Thailand. If I would be kind enough to send her US$1,500, she would pay me back on her return and would show her love and gratitude to me up close and personal. She included her photo in the message. It was of a woman with heavy pendant breasts precariously held up by a small top. She wore shorts and her bare stomach bulged out over her pants. She must have weighed at least a hundred kilos and was as black as the ace of spades. I would have thought that she needed to obtain a photo of a Thai if she wanted to pursue this line of work.

The only interesting thing that happened was when I corresponded with a Russian girl. Her photo was not posted on Lovelinks but she sent it to me when I wrote to her. It looked like someone had cut a picture out of a Russian copy of *Penthouse*. Super good looking, beautiful long legs and large breasts bursting out of a skimpy top. She proclaimed her love for me and knew that she had found her soul mate. By sheer good fortune she had a month off from her job and would be able to fly down to stay with me. The only problem was that the airfare cost US$1,100. She had saved US$200 and if I could just send her US$900, everything would be fine. I thought it over and suggested that she buy a bus ticket for as far as she could go for US$200 and then hitchhike the rest of the way. All she had to do was stick out one of those long legs and she would be here in no time.

I received a short, curt reply, not at all like those flowery love notes that she had been sending.

Maybe I needed to stick closer to home. I found a dating/ marriage service in Bangkok. My heart raced as I fired up the computer. Soon I would have the solution to my dilemma. No, wait, I couldn't do that. They would think it was an email from a crazy person. Imagine, a single man living in Thailand who couldn't get a date. Impossible. What kind of a nitwit could this guy be? I forged ahead and placed an advertisement in a weekly paper, *The Phuket Gazette*: OLDER AMERICAN MAN SEEKS LIVE-IN COMPANION. Two gay guys called me up.

'I was really looking for a girl.'

'I can take better care of you than any girl.'

The other one said, 'Try me, you'll like me.' He sounded like an old television advertisement.

Next was a fifty-year-old woman with more than a few miles on her. Tattoos of dragons peeked out at me from underneath her blouse. Then a reasonably attractive girl stopped by. As I led her through the house she seemed to be taking a mental inventory: computer, television, radio. I showed her to the door and hid the silverware. The next woman looked all right. As we talked, her list of requests mounted: she would need to borrow my car on occasion; I would have to buy new sheets, towels, a clothes cabinet and matching dresser for her; she could only cook a few days a week; she could sleep in the same bed with me but she had to keep her clothes on; if I wanted to have sex it would be only twice a month and it could not take too long; she needed 12,000 a month as she had to send money home.

I told her I would think it over.

'Don't you like me?' she said. I patted my faithful German Shepherd on the head.

'It's you and me, boy.'